Economy of Force: A Total Army, The Israel Defense Model

Charles E. Heller

Contents

Bibliographic Key Phrases 1

Publishing Information 3

Publisher's Note 5

Truth in Publishing (Disclosures) 7

Analytic Table of Contents 9
    Introduction 9
    The IDF: A Unique Force 9
    The Hova: The IDF's Manpower Pool 9
    The Officer Corps 9
    The Keva: The Regular Force 9
    The Miluimm: The Reserve Force 9
    The Women's Corps 10
    Force Structure and Mix 10
    Equipment 10
    Observations 10
    The Parts of the Model That Will Not Fit the U.S. Army 10
    The Relevant Aspects of the IDF 10
    Acceptance and Practice of a Total Army Concept 10
    Flow-through System 11
    Enlisted Service Required Prior to Commissioning 11
    National Service 11
    Significant Equipment Modernization Through Modification 11
    Peacetime Missions That Are Domestic Nation Building 11
    Joint Structure of the IDF 11
    Youthful Senior Leadership 11
    Brigade as the Basic Building Block of the Army's Force Structure 12
    Conclusions 12

Most Important Passages 13
    Passage 1 13
    Passage 2 13
    Passage 3 13
    Passage 4 14
    Passage 5 14
    Passage 6 14
    Passage 7 15

Condensed Matter 17
    Parts of the Model That Will Not Fit the U.S. Army: 19

About the Author 23

Historical Context 25

Abbreviations 27

Browsable Glossary 29

Timeline 31

Abstracts 33
    ELI5 33
    Scientific-Style Abstract 33
    For Complete Idiots Only 33

Learning Aids 35
    Mnemonic (acronym) 35
    Mnemonic (speakable) 35
    Mnemonic (singable) 35
    Three Conversation Starters 36

Introspection 37
    Self-Analysis 37
    Struggle session 37

Bibliographic Key Phrases

IDF; Citizen Army; Total Army; Military Model; Israeli Defense; Reserve Army; Army Restructuring; Military Innovation; Defense Budget; Peacetime Missions; Army Doctrine; Joint Structure;

Publishing Information

(c) 2024 Nimble Books LLC

ISBN: 978-1-60888-349-3

Nimble Books LLC ~ NimbleBooks.com

Humans and models making books richer, more diverse, and more surprising.

Publisher's Note

The post-Cold War world is a new and uncertain landscape, and the U.S. Army is grappling with the challenges of downsizing while remaining a formidable force. This report delves into the unique world of the Israel Defense Force (IDF), an army that has consistently mobilized rapidly and won its wars against overwhelming odds. The IDF, a citizen army with a massive reserve component, offers valuable insights for restructuring the U.S. Army and maximizing its effectiveness in a time of shrinking budgets and manpower.

This document explores the IDF's integrated force structure, its innovative approach to training and equipping, and its emphasis on peacetime missions that contribute to national development. The report provides an in-depth examination of the IDF's organizational structure, focusing on its active and reserve components, its officer corps, and its unique role in Israeli society. It delves into the IDF's reliance on equipment modernization through modification, highlighting its cost-saving practices and its remarkable ability to adapt and enhance existing weapons systems.

This report is a must-read for anyone interested in the future of the U.S. Army. Whether you are a researcher, policymaker, or simply a concerned citizen, this document provides a compelling case study of a successful model for a modern, adaptable, and cost-effective military force. The report offers valuable lessons for the U.S. Army as it navigates the complexities of the 21st century security environment, and it provides a unique perspective on the potential for innovation and efficiency in the face of resource constraints.

Truth in Publishing (Disclosures)

This document is a fascinating glimpse into the inner workings of the Israel Defense Force (IDF), a military that is often cited as a model for other countries. It's a valuable resource for anyone interested in the IDF or in modern military organization and doctrine. However, a discerning reader might be left with a few questions.

First, the paper's language is a bit dry and academic. It's not exactly light-hearted or entertaining, as the abstract suggests. The writer tends to over-rely on acronyms (Keva, Hova, Miluimm), which might leave some readers scratching their heads. And the use of the term "Miluimnicks" for reservists? Let's just say it's not exactly catchy.

Second, the paper is heavy on facts and details, which is good, but it doesn't always provide a strong narrative or make compelling arguments. For example, while the author highlights the IDF's emphasis on integrating active and reserve forces, he doesn't fully explain how this integration has shaped the IDF's strategic thinking or its operational effectiveness.

Third, the paper is a bit repetitive. It's like the author keeps driving home the point about the IDF's focus on cost-effectiveness, but the examples he uses to illustrate this point—upgrading old equipment, relying on the reserve—start to feel a little like a broken record.

Finally, the paper's attempt to draw parallels between the IDF and the U.S. Army isn't always convincing. Sure, the U.S. Army could learn from the IDF's experience, but the author doesn't always make a strong case for how specific IDF practices would work in the U.S. context.

Overall, the paper is informative, but it's a bit dry and repetitive. If the goal was to write a light-hearted and engaging piece, the author missed the mark. However, the paper is a valuable resource for anyone looking for detailed information about the IDF.

Analytic Table of Contents

Introduction

The author argues that the Israel Defense Force (IDF) provides a model for the post-Cold War U.S. Army. He analyzes the IDF and concludes that certain aspects of its force structure, equipment modernization, and peacetime missions could serve as a model for the U.S. Army.

The IDF: A Unique Force

The IDF is a unique force shaped by the constant threat to its national security. It is a reserve army, unlike other modern armies, and has evolved through a series of wars. The author describes the IDF's organizational structure, highlighting the General Staff, the Army, the Navy, the Air Force, and the territorial commands. He explains the integration of the IDF's active and reserve forces, with the reserve comprising 82.6 percent of the force.

The Hova: The IDF's Manpower Pool

The IDF draws its manpower from a mandatory service, the Hova, or national service, with all citizens required to perform military service or an alternative. The author explains the induction process, the mandatory service requirement for men and women, and the various exemption programs for religious and other categories. He outlines the intense training program, emphasizing the emphasis on combat survival skills and the minimal time devoted to drill and ceremony. The author also discusses the selection process for potential officers, highlighting the requirement of enlisted service prior to commissioning.

The Officer Corps

The IDF's officer corps is composed of both active duty officers (Keva) and reserve officers (Miluimm). The author emphasizes the unique characteristics of this corps, including the requirement of enlisted service prior to commissioning and the preference for youthful leadership. He discusses the challenges of attracting qualified officers to the Keva and the benefits of the flow-through system, which integrates active and reserve forces.

The Keva: The Regular Force

The Keva, the IDF's regulars, constitute a small but critical element of the force, comprising less than 10 percent of the total. The author explains the role of the Keva, which includes long-range planning, training, research and development, and the distribution and maintenance of materiel. He highlights the Keva's responsibility for the combat readiness of the reserve force, emphasizing the importance of a full-time cadre to support the Miluimm units.

The Miluimm: The Reserve Force

The Miluimm, comprising 82.6 percent of the IDF, represents the heart of the force. The author details the role of the Miluimm, explaining how it mobilizes, trains, and prepares for combat. He emphasizes the importance of the

Miluimm unit as an extended family, with a close-knit community of soldiers who live and train together. The author also explores the unique characteristics of the Miluimm, such as the reliance on Keva cadre for administration and training, and the mobilization procedures.

The Women's Corps

The author examines the role of women in the IDF, highlighting the limitations imposed by law and the changing roles women are taking in both combat and non-combat roles. He explains the challenges faced by women in the IDF, such as limited senior positions and the need to adapt to a male-dominated environment. He also discusses the opportunities for women to serve in non-traditional roles, especially within the Miluimm.

Force Structure and Mix

The author analyzes the IDF's force structure and mix, focusing on the brigade as the basic building block of the force. He discusses the different types of brigades, including armored, infantry, and artillery brigades, and explains the organization of divisions, which function primarily as brigade group headquarters. He also examines the manning levels of various units, highlighting the emphasis on cadre manning and the use of Keva personnel to support reserve units.

Equipment

The IDF has a unique approach to equipment, emphasizing cost-savings and modifications over new acquisitions. The author details the IDF's extensive inventory of modified equipment, including World War II half-tracks, Centurion tanks, and M-48A5 tanks. He explains how the IDF has modified captured Soviet equipment, demonstrating its ingenuity in using existing assets. The author also discusses the development of new weapons systems, such as the Merkava tank, and the importance of a vibrant defense industry in supporting modernization efforts.

Observations

The author makes a number of observations about the IDF, highlighting its successes and challenges. He emphasizes the importance of the IDF's integrated force structure, its commitment to modernization through modification, and its willingness to adapt to a changing environment. He also acknowledges the limitations of the IDF model, particularly in relation to the American cultural context.

The Parts of the Model That Will Not Fit the U.S. Army

The author identifies several aspects of the IDF model that are unlikely to be adopted by the U.S. Army, including mandatory conscription, the legal restrictions on women in combat, and the paramilitary youth organization (GADNA).

The Relevant Aspects of the IDF

The author outlines a number of relevant aspects of the IDF model that could be applied to the U.S. Army, including the acceptance of a Total Army concept, a flow-through system, enlisted service required prior to commissioning, a national service program, equipment modernization through modification, peacetime missions, a joint organizational structure, youthful senior leadership, and the brigade as the basic building block of the Army's force structure.

Acceptance and Practice of a Total Army Concept

The IDF's integrated force structure, with a significant reserve component, provides a model for the U.S. Army to adapt its Total Army concept. The author argues for a more integrated and unified approach to the U.S. Army, with a focus on streamlining and eliminating duplication of effort. He suggests that the Army should move away from a separate National Guard and embrace a more unified Federal reserve force structure.

Flow-through System

The IDF's flow-through system, which integrates active and reserve forces, provides a model for the U.S. Army. The author advocates for a more seamless transition between active duty and reserve service, with a focus on maintaining continuity and ensuring that reserve units have the necessary skills and training.

Enlisted Service Required Prior to Commissioning

The IDF's requirement of enlisted service prior to commissioning offers a model for the U.S. Army. The author argues for the benefits of enlisted experience in officer training, emphasizing the importance of developing a strong NCO corps and providing a more holistic approach to leadership development.

National Service

The IDF's national service model, with its emphasis on military service and citizenship education, provides a framework for the U.S. Army to explore the benefits of national service. The author suggests adapting the model to address the unique challenges of the U.S. and proposes a new Civilian Conservation Corps (CCC) as a potential model for national service.

Significant Equipment Modernization Through Modification

The IDF's focus on modifying existing equipment provides a model for the U.S. Army to explore ways to extend the service life of its existing inventory. The author emphasizes the benefits of a robust research and development program focused on upgrading existing systems and developing cost-effective solutions.

Peacetime Missions That Are Domestic Nation Building

The IDF's involvement in domestic nation-building projects, including education, infrastructure development, and social services, provides a model for the U.S. Army to expand its role beyond traditional military missions. The author advocates for a broader understanding of the Army's role in society and suggests a variety of peacetime missions that could be undertaken by the Army, especially the Reserve component.

Joint Structure of the IDF

The IDF's joint organizational structure, with a unified command for all services, offers a model for the U.S. to streamline its defense establishment. The author advocates for a more integrated and collaborative approach to joint operations, with a focus on eliminating duplication of effort and improving efficiency.

Youthful Senior Leadership

The IDF's preference for youthful senior leadership provides a model for the U.S. Army to consider. The author argues for a more dynamic and innovative officer corps, with a focus on promoting and retaining younger and more experienced officers. He suggests a more competitive and meritocratic approach to promotions and a shorter length of service for officers.

Brigade as the Basic Building Block of the Army's Force Structure

The IDF's use of the brigade as the basic building block of its force structure offers a model for the U.S. Army to consider. The author argues that the brigade is a flexible and adaptable unit that is well-suited for the complexities of the new world order. He proposes a more brigade-centric force structure, with a greater emphasis on independent brigades and a streamlined division structure.

Conclusions

The author concludes that the IDF model offers a number of valuable lessons for the U.S. Army, particularly in a time of declining defense budgets and a changing security environment. He emphasizes the need for a more integrated and unified force structure, with a focus on efficiency, cost-effectiveness, and a broader understanding of the Army's role in society. He encourages a more innovative and forward-thinking approach to leadership and a more collaborative approach to joint operations.

Most Important Passages

Passage 1

In seeking to survive as a credible deterrent force in the wake of cold war demobilization, U.S. Army senior leaders may find in the Israel Defense Force (IDF), or Tzava Haganah L'Yisrael, a model of an army which has always operated in an economy of force environment. With this force Israel has rapidly mobilized and always won its wars. A significant reason for both economy of force and for success lies in its reserve. A reserve one might add, that has the capability to rapidly mobilize and, without post-mobilization training, achieve success in combat. The U.S. Army does not require activation of hardly any of its Reserve Components (RC) in the approximately 24 hours the IDF requires, but as the Active Component (AC) becomes smaller, it would seem to require an increase in the missions and mobilization readiness of its RC. Part of the solution to the U.S. Army's challenge of downsizing at the end of the cold war while retaining an adequate force to accomplish anticipated missions is a new approach to force structure and mix, manning and equipping, and peacetime missions by using selected aspects of the IDF model for the restructuring that needs to take place.

Reason: This passage sets the context for the remainder of the article, and highlights the key takeaways the author hopes the reader will glean from his analysis of the IDF. The author introduces the idea that the IDF could serve as a model for a post-Cold War U.S. Army, particularly in the context of force structure and mix, manning and equipping, and peacetime missions.

Passage 2

No other modern army can duplicate the factors that influence and mold the IDF. Certainly culturally, politically, economically, and geographically the country has little in common with America except for being a democracy and sharing many Western cultural traits. Also, the imminent possibility and nearness of the threat posed by the likes of brutal dictators Saddam Hussein and Hafez al-Asad have never been duplicated in the Western hemisphere. However, some elements in the nature of the IDF may provide a U.S. peacetime army facing significant troop reductions and budget cuts, ideas to improve the mobilization and combat readiness of its Total Army force structure, keep its technological edge, maintain end strength, and become an decisive force in revitalizing the society it serves.

Reason: This passage provides crucial information about the context of the IDF. It acknowledges the significant differences between the United States and Israel, but underscores the relevance of certain aspects of the IDF's system to a downsizing U.S. Army. This sets up the core argument for the author's analysis, highlighting the potential value of examining the IDF as a model for the U.S. military.

Passage 3

Given this force structure, the most critical and unique aspect of the IDF is the Miluimm, which is "its most important operational component rather than just being an appendage to the regular force." Driven by economy of resources in dollars and manpower, the IDF developed an immediately deployable reserve which today comprises 82.6 percent (494,000) of its total military strength of 598,000. The regular force numbers 104,000, of which 88,000 are compulsory service soldiers. These are stunning figures and percentages when one considers the threat and the small margin between victory or defeat for a nation the size of New Jersey.!

Reason: This passage is important because it spotlights the unique strength of the IDF: its reliance on a massive and readily deployable reserve force. This key element differentiates the IDF from other armies and makes it a potentially valuable model for the United States. The author stresses the significance of the reserve's size and capability, emphasizing its role as a critical component of the IDF's success.

Passage 4

The IDF's manpower pool for the Keva and Miluimm is the Hova, compulsory or national service. From these ranks flow men and women into the Keva and Miluimm. Every Israeli citizen is required to perform military service or an alternative. A nationwide announcement is made every month by birth date for those youth who have reached their 18th birthday. About 92 percent of all males and 60 percent of all females are inducted. The lower percentage for women can be attributed to the exemptions offered: marriage or engagement, religion, and less than 8 years of formal schooling. In addition, the mental and physical standards are higher for females than for their male counterparts. Standard exemptions for religion, conscientious objections, or physical disabilities are given to males although the latter must be extreme and many young people with handicaps still serve in the public sector. One of the most commonly used exemptions is for religion. A very large number of young men of military age are ultra-orthodox Jews attending Yeshiva (religious school). This exemption is a source of contention among secular Jews and is a serious weakness in sharing the military burden in National Service.

Reason: This passage provides a detailed description of the IDF's national service system, the Hova. The author explains the requirements, exemptions, and implications of this mandatory service for Israeli citizens. This understanding is crucial for appreciating the IDF's overall system, as it serves as the foundation for both the regular and reserve forces.

Passage 5

The only other source of commissioning in the IDF is through the ranks by a careful screening of Hova soldiers that begins at induction. Each soldier is subjected to extensive batteries of tests to determine his or her talents and leadership qualities. Those with the highest motivation and intelligence are usually placed in combat units and programmed for leadership training in all branches of the service. After basic training, those Hova soldiers who by testing, observation, motivation, and desire indicate officer potential are selected for further training. They enter a rigorous program with no guarantee of a commission. There is additional schooling in the branch of service, decided again by batteries of tests, interviews, personal preferences, and needs of the IDF.

Reason: This passage delves into the unique commissioning process of the IDF, highlighting its emphasis on meritocratic selection and practical experience. The author describes the rigorous process of screening, training, and evaluation, emphasizing that officers in the IDF gain valuable experience through enlisted service. This system contrasts with the traditional military academy model and offers a distinct perspective on officer development.

Passage 6

The IDF, as an institution, has a very positive attitude toward its reserve. Obviously, with the bulk of the force being citizen-soldiers, the emphasis has to be there. Part of the IDF emphasis is the reliance on the integration of its components to mold an affordable deterrent force. The IDF's mix of Keva, Hova, and Miluimm individuals and units within the force structure is a major ingredient for the success of the force in combat. The assignment of Keva soldiers to reserve units is accepted as the norm and does not affect career progression or signal a terminal assignment as is many times the case in the U.S. Army. In fact the IDF Keva officer's assignment to reserve units may even enhance advancement. Keva officers can be assigned down to battalion level in staff positions in reserve units. This cadre appears to be placed in IDF reserve units with no particular motive other than finding the best officer for the assignment. The element of stability, experience, and knowledge of full-time manning personnel is one factor that influences battlefield results for Miluimm units. However, Miluimm officers who show promise can and do command at brigade and division level as well as serve in staff positions and offices throughout the Keva.

Reason: This passage highlights the importance of integration between the different components of the IDF and the positive attitude towards the reserve force. The author describes how the IDF's system fosters a sense of unity and shared responsibility, ensuring that the reserve force is not seen as a secondary entity but rather a vital part of the overall military structure. This emphasizes the key aspects of a Total Army concept that the author seeks to promote for the U.S. Army.

Passage 7

The IDF has never had the U.S. Army's misfortune to be cast aside after a war because the threat to Israel has remained constant. In fact, after the last major war in 1973, "peace" brought a significant expansion of the force. The cost to the small nation has been tremendous. No one could ever suggest that Israel could afford, both financially and in the lost civilian productivity of scarce manpower, a large standing army constantly mobilized for war. Even with U.S. materiel and financial support, this full-time readiness state is not attainable.

Reason: This passage illustrates the unique context in which the IDF operates, highlighting the constant threat to Israel's national security. The author describes the necessity of maintaining a strong defense posture, even during periods of peace, and explains how the IDF's reliance on its reserve force allows it to balance its defense needs with economic and social realities. This underscores the importance of the IDF model for a U.S. Army seeking to optimize its resources in a changing world.

Condensed Matter

This report examines the Israel Defense Force (IDF) as a model for the U.S. Army in a post-Cold War world. The author argues that the IDF is a model of an army that has always operated in an "economy of force" environment, successfully mobilizing and winning wars despite limited resources. The IDF's strength lies in its reliance on reserve forces, which are integrated into the overall force structure and rapidly mobilized without extensive post-mobilization training. The report examines the IDF's organization, force structure, and equipment, highlighting its strengths and unique features. The author concludes that selected aspects of the IDF model could be useful for restructuring the post-Cold War U.S. Army, including adopting a total force concept, integrating active and reserve components, requiring enlisted service before commissioning, and implementing national service programs.

The Israel Defense Force (IDF) is organized under a single General Staff (Hamateh Hakiala) for the Army, Air Force, and Navy. The Army (Zahal) is commanded by the Chief of Staff (Ra'Mat'KaI), who functions in a role similar to the U.S. Chairman of the Joint Chiefs in wartime. In peacetime the Navy (Heyl Hayam) and Air Force (Heyl Havir) are controlled by their respective commanders, who report to the Chief of Staff in wartime. The General Staff currently has five branches: Operations, Quartermaster (Logistics), Manpower (Personnel), Intelligence, and Planning. Reporting directly to the Chief of Staff are a number of Commands: Communications Command, Civil Defense, the NAHAL or Fighting Pioneer Youth (NoarHalutz Lochaim), and the Ground Forces Command. Israel is divided into three IDF territorial commands, Northern, Central, and Southern. These commands provide the administrative and operational framework for the IDF. Each territorial command has a Major General commanding and deputy staff officers responsible for operations, training, and supply.

The Israel Defense Force (IDF) is a reserve army with 82.6% of its strength in the reserves (Miluimm). The mix of Keva (active duty), Hova (compulsory service), and Miluimm is unique and critical to the IDF's success. Keva soldiers are integrated into reserve units, serving in staff positions down to battalion level, bringing stability and experience to the Miluimm. Miluimm officers can command at brigade and division level and serve in staff positions throughout the Keva. The IDF's integration of its components differs from the U.S. Army's Total Force Policy by: 1) the IDF's emphasis on a single army structure, where all components are interchangeable in battle, whereas the U.S. Army has a more distinct division between the Active Component and Reserve Components; 2) the IDF's emphasis on a true flow-through system, where soldiers transition seamlessly from active duty to reserve service, whereas the U.S. Army has a more fragmented system; 3) the IDF's requirement for enlisted service prior to commissioning, whereas the U.S. Army offers multiple paths to commissioning.

Hova, the IDF's compulsory service, forms the core of Israel's manpower pool. Every Israeli citizen is required to perform military service or an alternative. Approximately 92 percent of all males and 60 percent of all females are inducted. The lower percentage for women can be attributed to exemptions offered: marriage or engagement, religion, and less than 8 years of formal schooling. [ ]

The standard service is 3 years for men and 20 months for females. [ ] There are nonmilitary options for religious women who wish to serve and there are also special arrangements for those youth attending Yeshiva. [ ] Open to high school graduates, the inductees are given a 1-year deferment and enrolled in one of 15 special religious schools called "yeshivothesder." The youth serve two 1-year periods in the army and two 1-year periods at their studies. When their Hova service is completed, they finish their reserve service with no special privileges. [ ]

New Hova recruits are all sent to Ba'K'UM, the Hebrew acronym for the "Absorption and Assortment Base." Prior to arrival, while still civilians, all conscripts have undergone their initial extensive medical and psychiatric examinations, and batteries of intelligence and aptitude testing. [ ] Conscripts are then separated into 14 classifications. [ ]

Basic training in the IDF is required of everyone, even those earmarked for the Navy or Air Force. The training has so many different tracks that it appears to an outsider that it is tailored to each individual who enters the IDF. [ ] The only exemptions for some parts of the demanding combat training under extremely harsh conditions are given to those individuals with very low physical or mental standards. [ ] Training dropouts are recycled until they complete the course assigned. There is no waste of any resources, especially human. [ ]

Very little time in any of the training schedules is devoted to drill and ceremony. The emphasis is on combat survival skills with large blocks of instruction given to weapons qualification and physical fitness. The IDF conducts much of its training in the field and with live fire whenever possible. [ ] The purpose of making training as realistic as possible is because the vast majority of recruits will enter the Miluimm. [ ]

Inductees, if qualified, have the opportunity to select specialties. [ ] A number of special qualification jobs exist in the Intelligence corps. Many recruits attempt to join elite units like the paratroops. Any of these voluntary career options extend the Hova service obligation because of the additional training and the cost of the investment in that individual. [ ] Officer candidacy, for example, requires one additional year of active service. Those who wish to volunteer for elite units or officer training can only do so if they are in the upper six levels on the classification scale. [ ]

The IDF emphasizes enlisted experience prior to commissioning, meaning no one can become an officer without having trained and served as an enlisted soldier. This differs from the U.S. Army's system of commissioning, which offers multiple pathways, including military academies. In the IDF, the absence of academies is attributed to the "egalitarian ethos of Israeli life" and the belief that military academies imply "connotations of social inequality." The IDF believes that officers learn best from the ground up, which enables them to focus on cognitive skills in later training instead of basic combat survival skills.The Keva, or Permanent Service, is the IDF's regular force, comprised of a small cadre of primarily officers and NCOs. While the Keva represents a small percentage of the IDF's total strength, they are essential for training, long-range planning, maintenance of equipment, and supporting the reserves. Keva members are motivated by a desire to serve the nation, and they enjoy high pay and extensive benefits. However, they also face the challenges of constant danger, separation from family, and a heavy workload, even in peacetime. A crucial role of the Keva is to ensure the combat readiness of the reserve forces by providing support structure, long-range planning, training preparation for combat, research and development, and distribution and maintenance of all materiel. The Keva also provides a significant amount of technical specialists who are essential for operating and maintaining the IDF's equipment.

The Miluimm (IDF reserves) comprises 82.6 percent of the IDF's total strength, with 494,000 reservists. This makes it the most important operational component. Reservists are considered citizen-soldiers and are integrated into the IDF's total force structure. The Keva (permanent service) officers and NCOs are intimately familiar with their reserve forces. Many Miluimm units enter combat alongside Keva units. The length of active duty for a Miluimm soldier varies greatly depending on the political climate of the region, with a minimum of 45 days annually. The IDF utilizes reservists in a variety of peacetime missions such as riot control, border patrol, and national development. The Miluimm soldier's primary focus is combat survival skills, as they may be called upon to enter combat without additional training. Every soldier, including reservists, receives extensive training in combat survival skills.

Women serve in the IDF but have a shorter service obligation than men (20 months vs 3 years). While they are typically barred from combat positions, shortages of manpower have led to their inclusion in formerly male-dominated roles, particularly in the reserves. They also serve in nonmilitary roles such as teaching and aiding new immigrants. While women have begun to break through into officer ranks, they still face challenges in achieving senior leadership positions in the IDF.

The basic combat maneuver formation in the IDF is the brigade. There are three types of brigades: armor, infantry, and artillery. Divisions exist and are similar to any other nation's formations when conducting operations. The IDF has three armored division equivalents in the Keva. Upon mobilization, each is fleshed out with one mechanized infantry brigade. The Miluimm contains nine armored division equivalents composed of from two to three armored brigades. There are ten cadre Miluimm regional infantry brigades assigned specific border sectors commanded by the three regional headquarters, North, Central, and South. Each unit has its own armory. Training might be conducted at the armory or at special training centers. Other periods of active duty may find the Miluimm unit relieving a Keva unit on border patrol or performing internal security patrols or familiarizing on a new weapon.The IDF's approach to equipment modernization is one of unique ingenuity and cost-saving. Faced with limited budgets and a small manpower pool, they prioritize reusing and modifying existing equipment rather than purchasing new gear.

For example, the IDF still uses over 4,400 World War II M2/3 half tracks, many salvaged from scrap yards in Western

Europe. These vehicles have been heavily modified and upgraded to meet the demands of modern warfare. The IDF also fields 1,080 British Centurion World War II tanks that have been modernized with a new engine, American automatic transmission, and a 105mm gun.

They have further modernized Korean War era M-48A5 tanks to the point that they are essentially M-60s, upgrading the gun, fire control system, and engine. This includes utilizing captured Soviet equipment, including T-54/55 tanks, which have been fitted with a 105mm gun, a U.S. power train, air conditioning, and Western European machine guns.

The IDF's strategy highlights the potential for cost savings by utilizing and modifying existing equipment, demonstrating that a smaller army can still be an effective fighting force through intelligent use of resources. The author describes the Israel Defense Force (IDF) as a model for the post-Cold War U.S. Army, noting its strengths in maintaining an effective fighting force with over 80% of its total force in the reserve, through a system that conserves money, manpower, and time.

The author highlights the IDF's integrated force structure, where soldiers and units are interchangeable in battle. The IDF's reliance on reserves allows for a "citizens'" army, solving budgetary problems and ensuring a more affordable force structure. He also emphasizes the importance of the IDF's acceptance and practice of a Total Army concept, its flow-through system of active to reserve service, its requirement of enlisted service prior to commissioning, its implementation of National Service, and its focus on significant equipment modernization through modification.

Parts of the Model That Will Not Fit the U.S. Army:

- **Peacetime Military Conscription:** The American public would likely reject conscription, favoring the current All-Volunteer Force model.
- **Limited Role for Women in Combat:** American women would likely oppose the IDF's restrictions on female participation in combat roles.
- **Paramilitary Youth Organization:** The GADNA, a paramilitary youth scouting organization, would be unlikely to gain acceptance in the United States due to concerns about indoctrination.
- **Officer-Led Army:** The U.S. Army traditionally relies on a strong NCO corps as the backbone of its force, making an officer-led structure impractical. ## Relevant Aspects of the IDF:

The report, "Economy of Force: A Total Army, The Israel Defense Force Model," by Charles E. Heller, proposes that certain aspects of the IDF could be useful for a post-cold war U.S. Army. These aspects are:

- **Acceptance and practice of a Total Army concept:** The IDF demonstrates the effectiveness of integrating active and reserve forces into a single, cohesive unit, rather than viewing them as separate entities. This allows for efficient utilization of resources and ensures a higher level of combat readiness.
- **Flow-through system (active to reserve service):** The IDF's system of having soldiers serve in active duty followed by reserve service ensures continuity and consistency in training and skillsets. It also helps in maintaining a large, well-trained reserve force.
- **Enlisted service required prior to commissioning:** This system emphasizes practical experience and reinforces the importance of leadership stemming from a strong understanding of the enlisted ranks.
- **National Service:** While not directly transferable to the U.S., the IDF's national service model showcases the benefits of requiring all citizens to contribute to national defense, either through military service or alternative programs. This promotes civic duty and reinforces the concept of shared responsibility.
- **Significant equipment modernization through modification:** The IDF exemplifies the value of maximizing existing equipment through continuous modification and upgrading, which not only extends the lifespan of assets but also stimulates the domestic defense industry.
- **Peacetime missions that are domestic nation-building in nature:** The IDF is actively involved in civilian projects like education, social development, and environmental conservation, demonstrating the potential of the military to contribute to societal well-being beyond warfare.
- **Joint organizational structure of the IDF:** The IDF's single, unified General Staff for all branches of service represents a model for promoting greater interservice cooperation and eliminating redundancies, ultimately leading to more efficient resource allocation.
- **Youthful senior officer leadership:** The IDF prioritizes innovative thinking by fostering a younger officer corps, encouraging early retirement for senior officers and promoting a culture of constant change and adaptation.

- **Brigade as the basic building block of the Army's force structure:** The IDF's reliance on brigades as the primary combat unit emphasizes flexibility and adaptability in a rapidly changing world, allowing for more tailored deployments and effective command and control.

These aspects are presented not as a direct blueprint for the U.S. Army, but rather as a set of ideas worth considering as the U.S. faces a new era of budget constraints and evolving security threats. The report acknowledges the differences between the two societies, highlighting areas where the IDF model may be unsuitable for the United States. It emphasizes the need for innovative thinking and adapting solutions to fit the specific context of the U.S. Army. The IDF model is a valuable example of how a small nation can field a powerful and effective military force. The report argues that the U.S. Army can learn from this model as it adapts to a post-Cold War environment. Key takeaways from the IDF model include the value of:

- **Total Army concept:** The IDF operates with a single force structure where regular and reserve components are fully integrated.
- **Flow-through system:** Regular army soldiers transition to reserve units, maintaining training and education standards.
- **Enlisted service before commissioning:** All officers must first serve as enlisted soldiers, fostering a strong NCO corps.
- **National service:** Compulsory military service is a requirement of Israeli citizenship, contributing to a strong and well-trained force.
- **Equipment modernization:** The IDF maximizes its defense budget by constantly upgrading and modifying existing equipment.
- **Peacetime missions:** The IDF plays a significant role in nation-building and domestic affairs, demonstrating its value beyond combat.
- **Joint organizational structure:** The IDF operates with a single General Staff for all services, promoting efficiency and collaboration.
- **Youthful senior leadership:** The IDF prioritizes fresh thinking and innovation by encouraging early retirement and promotion.
- **Brigade as the basic force structure:** Brigades, rather than divisions, provide flexibility and agility in deploying forces.

The author acknowledges that certain aspects of the IDF model are not suitable for the U.S. Army, such as mandatory conscription and the restrictions on women in combat. However, he emphasizes the importance of considering the adaptable and relevant aspects of the IDF model, particularly in light of the changing global environment and budget constraints. ## Economy of Force: A Total Army, The Israel Defense Force Model

This report examines the Israel Defense Force (IDF) as a model for the post-Cold War U.S. Army, particularly its reliance on a reserve force in a limited-resource environment. The author, Colonel Charles E. Heller, argues that the IDF's success in rapidly mobilizing and winning wars is due in part to its integrated total force structure, which includes a significant reserve component (Miluimm). This structure is compared to the U.S. Army's Active Component (AC) and Reserve Components (RC), particularly the Army Reserve (USAR) and the National Guard (ARNG). Heller proposes that a restructuring of the U.S. Army based on the IDF model could be beneficial.

Key Aspects of the IDF Model

Heller identifies several key aspects of the IDF that could be relevant to the U.S. Army:

- **Total Army Concept:** The IDF's integrated structure, with seamless transitions between active and reserve service, provides a cost-effective solution for a small nation facing a constant threat. This challenges the U.S. Army's traditional separation of AC and RC forces.
- **Flow-through System:** The IDF's system, where active duty personnel eventually transition to the reserve, helps maintain training standards and integration between components. The USAR could benefit from this approach.
- **Enlisted Service before Commissioning:** The IDF requires enlisted service for all officers, ensuring a strong foundation in basic soldiering skills. This practice could improve leadership within the U.S. Army.
- **National Service:** While conscription may not be acceptable in the U.S., the IDF's emphasis on national service, including alternative programs, could inspire a new approach to civilian service.
- **Equipment Modernization:** The IDF's practice of modifying and upgrading existing equipment demonstrates a resourceful approach to budget constraints. This emphasizes the importance of continuous modernization for

the U.S. Army.
- **Peacetime Missions:** The IDF's involvement in domestic nation-building tasks underscores the Army's potential role beyond purely military operations. This challenges the U.S. Army to broaden its mission set.
- **Joint Structure:** The IDF's unified General Staff for all services offers a model for a more integrated, cost-efficient U.S. military.
- **Youthful Leadership:** The IDF's emphasis on younger senior leadership promotes innovation and adaptability, something the U.S. Army could benefit from.
- **Brigade as the Basic Unit:** The IDF's reliance on brigades as the primary combat element offers greater flexibility and adaptability for a smaller, more agile Army.

Endnotes:

The endnotes provide essential context and support for the main argument. They reference a variety of sources, including academic studies, military journals, and government reports, to back up Heller's observations and analysis of the IDF. The endnotes highlight the complexities of the IDF system, showcasing its unique evolution and the various factors influencing its structure and operation. Furthermore, they provide a deeper understanding of the cultural, political, and historical context within which the IDF operates, enriching the report's analysis and strengthening its credibility.

About the Author

Colonel Charles E. Heller is the U.S. Army Reserve Advisor to the Strategic Studies Institute, U.S. Army War College. He holds a B.A. in history from Hofstra University and an M.A. and Ph.D. in U.S. history from the University of Massachusetts/Amherst. He has served on active duty with the 8th Infantry Division in Germany, and his last assignment was as Chief, Mobilization Training Division, U.S. Army Reserve Personnel Center. Colonel Heller is the author of numerous articles on military history and co-editor of *America's First Battles*, published by the University Press of Kansas.

His interest in the Israel Defense Force (IDF) stemmed from intellectual curiosity and the post-Cold War era's drastic reduction in U.S. defense spending, a situation that parallels Israel's own history of maintaining a credible deterrent force while operating in an economy-of-force environment. Colonel Heller's analysis of the IDF highlights the force's unique reliance on its reserve components and its adoption of a total force concept, which he believes hold valuable lessons for restructuring the U.S. military for the twenty-first century.

In his work, Colonel Heller draws on the pioneering work of theorists like Major General J.F.C. Fuller and the writings of leading historians and commentators like Edward Luttwak, Ze'ev Schiff, and Reuven Gal.

Colonel Heller's insightful examination of the IDF has earned him a reputation as a keen observer and thoughtful analyst of military affairs. His work is consistently insightful and engaging, offering a valuable perspective on the challenges and opportunities faced by the U.S. Army in the evolving global environment.

Historical Context

The 1992 study, "Economy of Force: A Total Army, The Israel Defense Force Model," by Charles E. Heller, Colonel, US Army Reserve, was written during the period of significant reduction of the US Army after the end of the Cold War. It was the time when the US Army needed to find new models for its force structure and mix, manning and equipping, and peacetime missions. While the historical context for Heller's writing may seem straightforward, the study is actually a complex examination of a historical moment in time, particularly during the Cold War.

The study is also significant for its place in the discourse about the role of the US Army after the Cold War. Heller's study focuses on the Israel Defense Force (IDF), a model of an army that has always operated in an economy of force environment.

Heller's study has resurfaced the debate about the proper mix of active and reserve forces. His work proposes that a new approach to force structure and mix, manning and equipping, and peacetime missions, could be developed by using selected aspects of the IDF model for the restructuring that needs to take place in the post-Cold War US Army.

It is unclear, however, whether the study is more relevant today, especially in the context of recent events, than it was at the time of its publication. The rise of non-state actors and the shifting nature of warfare in the 21st century might render the study less relevant in its emphasis on a traditional interstate threat and traditional military model. Nevertheless, the study's focus on the value of reserve forces and the importance of cost-efficiency within a military force, are both increasingly relevant to a US Army facing budgetary constraints.

One could argue that Heller's study is still important as future decades unroll. Its focus on the need for national service and its call for a more integrated army are issues that continue to be debated, particularly in an era of shrinking budgets and the need to find new ways to maintain national security. Heller's study should be seen as part of the ongoing conversation about the future of the US Army and the role of the military in a changing world.

Abbreviations

AC
Active Component

AMSA
Area Maintenance Support Activities

ARNG
Army National Guard

AT
Annual Training

Ba'K'UM
Absorption and Assortment Base

CHEN
Charm (Women's Corps)

CINC
Commander-in-Chief

CONUS
Continental United States

CRAF
Civilian Reserve Aircraft

CCC
Civilian Conservation Corps

CSS
Combat Service Support

GADNA
Youth Battalions ("Bow and Arrow")

Hamateh Hakiala
General Staff

Heyl Havir
Air Force

Heyl Hayam
Navy

Heyl Nashim
Women's Corps

Hova
Compulsory Service

IDF
Israel Defense Force

IMA
Individual Mobilization Augmentee

IRR
Individual Ready Reserve

lET
Initial Entry Training

Keva
Permanent Service

MATES/ECS
Mobilization and Training Sites/Equipment Concentration Sites

Miluimm
Reserve units and individuals

NAHAL
Fighting Pioneer Youth (NoarHalutz Lochaim)

NCO
Noncommissioned officer

ORC
Organized Reserve Corps

RC
Reserve Components

TRADOC
Training and Doctrine Command

TTAD
Temporary Tours of Active Duty

USAR
U.S. Army Reserve

TDA
Table of Distribution and Allowances

Browsable Glossary

Keva This term is a Hebrew acronym for *Permanent Service*, which refers to the regular or full-time components of the IDF, as opposed to reservists (Miluimm). The Keva is responsible for training, planning, and equipping the IDF.

Miluimm A Hebrew acronym for *Reserve*, this term refers to the reserve component of the IDF. Because of the IDF's structure, the Miluimm is not simply an appendage to the active forces, but its most important operational component.

Hova This Hebrew word refers to *Compulsory Service*, which applies to all Israelis who are required to perform national service in the IDF, including men and women. The Hova is the manpower pool for both the Keva and Miluimm.

GADNA This Hebrew acronym for *Youth Battalions* is a paramilitary organization that provides a certain amount of citizenship education for Israelis, instilling in youth a knowledge of the security situation and preparing them for their future Hova service.

NAHAL An acronym for *Fighting Pioneer Youth*, the NAHAL is a combination of military and agricultural training for youth, providing a way to maintain settlement security while farming the land.

CHEN This Hebrew acronym for *Charm* refers to the IDF's *Women's Corps*. It is commanded by a female brigadier general.

Tzava Haganah L'Yisrael This Hebrew phrase translates to *Israel Defense Force*, which is the official name of the armed forces of Israel.

Ra'Mat'KaI This Hebrew phrase translates to *Chief of Staff*, which is the highest position in the IDF.

Hamateh Hakiala This Hebrew phrase translates to *General Staff*. It is the single command structure responsible for all of the IDF's services: Army, Air Force, and Navy.

Heyl Hayam This Hebrew phrase translates to *Navy*.

Heyl Havir This Hebrew phrase translates to *Air Force*.

Yeshiva A Hebrew word referring to *religious schools* for Orthodox Jewish youth, students at these schools are typically exempt from military service.

Yom Kippur This Hebrew phrase translates to *Day of Atonement*, referring to the Jewish holiday on which the 1973 Arab-Israeli War began.

Merkava This Hebrew word translates to *Chariot*, referring to the Israeli-designed and manufactured main battle tank.

Haganah Merchavio This Hebrew phrase translates to *Combat Unit*.

Ba'K'UM This Hebrew acronym for *Absorption and Assortment Base* is the IDF training center where all conscripts receive their initial extensive medical and psychiatric examinations, batteries of intelligence and aptitude testing, and classification into 14 different categories.

Soltam Company A defense manufacturing company in Israel responsible for producing various weapons systems, including the L-33 self-propelled howitzer.

Cummins diesel engine A highly regarded brand of diesel engines used throughout the world, especially in commercial vehicles.

Torsion bar suspension A type of suspension system used in military vehicles, especially tanks, that provides a much more flexible and smooth ride.

Lance A British-made medium-range ballistic missile with nuclear capability.

Patriot An American-designed and manufactured long-range missile system designed to intercept incoming enemy missiles.

Super Sherman A modification of the M4 Sherman tank used during World War II, often featuring a 105mm gun.

Centurion A British-designed main battle tank used during World War II.

M-48 An American-designed main battle tank used extensively during the Korean War.

M-60 An American-designed main battle tank, its main gun is a 105mm cannon.

T-54/55 A Soviet-designed main battle tank, used in the IDF inventory.

T-67 A modified version of the T-54/55 tank.

Galil An Israeli-designed assault rifle.

M-110 A U.S.-designed self-propelled howitzer, which fires 203mm shells.

M-109 A U.S.-designed self-propelled howitzer.

M-2/3 A U.S.-designed half track armored personnel carrier used during World War II.

Posse Comitatus A Latin term for *Power of the County*, referring to a United States law that prohibits the use of the U.S. military for law enforcement purposes.

Task Force Smith A U.S. Army unit sent to Korea in 1950 at the beginning of the Korean War, the unit was sent in to fight the North Korean invasion, but was ill-prepared and suffered heavy losses.

Timeline

The IDF evolves from a small, volunteer army to a conscript force.

The IDF's structure is organized with a small cadre of regular forces and a large reserve.

The IDF is used to assimilate immigrants into Israeli society.

The IDF develops its own doctrine and tactics based on its experiences in the War for Independence.

The IDF introduces the Galil rifle.

The IDF modifies its equipment to suit its needs and resources.

The IDF creates the GADNA, a paramilitary youth organization.

The IDF fights the 1956 Suez Crisis.

The IDF fights the 1967 Six Day War.

The IDF introduces the Merkava tank.

The IDF fights the 1973 Yom Kippur War.

The IDF introduces the L-33 self-propelled artillery piece.

The IDF introduces the Patriot missile battery.

The IDF introduces the Merkava Mark III tank.

The IDF fights the 1982 Lebanon War.

The IDF introduces a new generation of Centurion tanks.

The IDF fights the First Intifada.

The IDF introduces the Merkava Mark IV tank.

The IDF faces a new threat from the Hamas and Islamic Jihad in the Second Intifada.

The IDF fights the Second Lebanon War.

The IDF engages in operations against Hezbollah and Hamas in Gaza.

The IDF modernizes its equipment and doctrine in preparation for future conflicts.

Abstracts

ELI5

This document talks about the Israeli army and how it's organized. It compares the Israeli army to the American army and talks about how the Israeli army has learned to fight effectively even though it is much smaller than its enemies.

Scientific-Style Abstract

This study examined the Israel Defense Force (IDF) as a model for the U.S. Army in a post-cold war era of reduced budgets. The IDF force structure and mix was analyzed for relevant aspects that might enhance the capability of the U.S. Army in a peacetime environment with dramatic funding and manpower constraints. After examining the IDF, its structure, force mix, weapons, officer corps, women's corps and missions, the conclusion reached is that some aspects of this force could serve as a model for the post-cold war U.S. Army. These aspects are: acceptance and practice of a Total Army concept, flow-through system (active to reserve service), enlisted service required prior to commissioning, national service, significant equipment modernization through modification, peacetime missions that are domestic nation building in nature, joint organizational structure of the IDF, youthful senior officer leadership, and the brigade as the basic building block of the Army's force structure. The Israeli army has many unique features, such as a large reserve force and a focus on national service, which might provide a model for the American Army in a time of shrinking budgets and changing military priorities. The study concludes that the American Army could benefit from adopting elements of the Israeli model such as the Total Force concept, flow-through system, mandatory service, and the use of a brigade as the basic building block.

For Complete Idiots Only

The IDF is Israel's army. It's a citizen army where almost everyone serves, but unlike the U.S., the IDF is mostly made up of reservists who are called up when needed. Because they're always on alert, they can mobilize quickly. This means they can respond to attacks without being totally unprepared. They use old equipment, but fix it up and keep it running, which helps them save money. They also have a program for young people that combines military and civilian duties, like building things and helping out in their communities. It's all about being ready for anything, and doing things cheaply and efficiently.

Learning Aids

Mnemonic (acronym)

IDF: Integrated, Deployable, Force

Mnemonic (speakable)

Hova soldier, Keva cadre, Miluimm reservist.

Mnemonic (singable)

>(To the tune of "My Bonnie Lies Over the Ocean")
>The IDF is a force to be reckoned with,
>Though small in size, its strength is sure.
>With Hova recruits and Keva cadre,
>The Miluimm reserve, a force secure.
>The IDF is always ready,
>To defend the land so dearly.
>With training rigorous,
>It's a force both courageous and serious.
>(Chorus)
>The IDF, a mighty force,
>Against all odds, it takes its course.
>With every soldier trained and true,
>It stands its ground, forever anew.
>The Merkava tank, a symbol of strength,
>A testament to Israeli ingenuity.
>With modified weapons and a spirit bold,
>The IDF story will forever be told.
>(Chorus)
>The IDF, a mighty force,
>Against all odds, it takes its course.

With every soldier trained and true,

It stands its ground, forever anew.

Three Conversation Starters

Here are three conversation starters related to the document AD-A251 603, "Economy of Force: A Total Army, The Israel Defense Force Model," by Charles E. Heller:

1. **"Have you heard about the Israeli Defense Force's reserve system? It's a model of efficiency, and it's got me thinking about how we could restructure our own military."** This starter introduces a topic that's likely to be relevant to anyone interested in national security or military affairs.
2. **"Did you know that the IDF trains its soldiers in a way that makes them immediately ready for combat? It's a fascinating approach, and I'm curious what lessons we can learn from it."** This starter focuses on a specific aspect of the IDF, likely to spark curiosity and discussion.
3. **"I just read an interesting article about the Israeli army and how they've managed to maintain a strong military despite budget constraints. It's got me thinking about how we can do the same in the US."** This starter emphasizes the practical implications of the IDF's approach, making it relevant to a wider audience.

Introspection

Self-Analysis

The original text of "Economy of Force: A Total Army, The Israel Defense Force Model" is a detailed study of the IDF and its relevance as a model for the post-Cold War U.S. Army. It exhaustively examines the IDF's organization, force structure, manpower pool, training, officer corps, equipment, and peacetime missions. This approach results in a lengthier, more comprehensive analysis, providing a deep dive into the intricacies of the IDF and its implications for the U.S. Army.

The condensed version, while losing some of the intricate details of the original, delivers the essence of Heller's argument. It retains the core analysis of the IDF as a model for a leaner, more flexible U.S. Army, highlighting key aspects like the Total Army concept, flow-through systems, and the importance of a robust reserve force. It also focuses on the IDF's approach to equipment modernization, peacetime missions, and youthful leadership. The condensed version prioritizes clear articulation of the relevant points and avoids unnecessary repetition, resulting in a more accessible and concise read for a broader audience.

Struggle session

This condensed version, though a valiant effort, still faces challenges. While aiming for accessibility, we lost some nuance, specifically regarding the complexities of the IDF's personnel system, the internal dynamics of its officer corps, and the intricacies of its equipment modernization program. We must strive to incorporate a greater degree of depth and complexity while remaining mindful of the need for clarity and conciseness. Additionally, the editorial team must ensure meticulous adherence to Chicago Manual of Style guidelines. We must also address potential sensitivities surrounding the topic of conscription and the role of women in the armed forces. To make this piece truly impactful, we need to explore ways to highlight the IDF's unique contributions to military thought and its role in shaping modern warfare doctrine.

AD-A251 603

SSI
Strategic Studies Institute
U.S. Army War College

ECONOMY OF FORCE: A TOTAL ARMY, THE ISRAEL DEFENSE FORCE MODEL

Charles E. Heller

This document has been approved for public release and sale; its distribution is unlimited.

UNCLASSIFIED
SECURITY CLASSIFICATION OF THIS PAGE

REPORT DOCUMENTATION PAGE

Form Approved
OMB No. 0704-0188

1a. REPORT SECURITY CLASSIFICATION UNCLASSIFIED	1b RESTRICTIVE MARKINGS	
2a. SECURITY CLASSIFICATION AUTHORITY	3 DISTRIBUTION / AVAILABILITY OF REPORT Approved for public release; distribution unlimited	
2b. DECLASSIFICATION / DOWNGRADING SCHEDULE		
4. PERFORMING ORGANIZATION REPORT NUMBER(S) ACN 92023	5 MONITORING ORGANIZATION REPORT NUMBER(S)	
6a. NAME OF PERFORMING ORGANIZATION Strategic Studies Institute	6b. OFFICE SYMBOL (If applicable) AWCI	7a. NAME OF MONITORING ORGANIZATION
6c. ADDRESS (City, State, and ZIP Code) U.S. Army War College Carlisle Barracks, PA 17013-50505		7b. ADDRESS (City, State, and ZIP Code)
8a. NAME OF FUNDING / SPONSORING ORGANIZATION	8b. OFFICE SYMBOL (If applicable)	9 PROCUREMENT INSTRUMENT IDENTIFICATION NUMBER
8c. ADDRESS (City, State, and ZIP Code)	10 SOURCE OF FUNDING NUMBERS	

PROGRAM ELEMENT NO.	PROJECT NO.	TASK NO.	WORK UNIT ACCESSION NO.

11. TITLE (Include Security Classification)
Economy of Force: A Total Army, The Israel Defense Model (U)

12. PERSONAL AUTHOR(S)
Heller, Charles E.

13a. TYPE OF REPORT Final	13b. TIME COVERED FROM ____ TO ____	14. DATE OF REPORT (Year, Month, Day) 1992 Mar 15	15. PAGE COUNT 54

16. SUPPLEMENTARY NOTATION

17. COSATI CODES			18. SUBJECT TERMS (Continue on reverse if necessary and identify by block number)
FIELD	GROUP	SUB-GROUP	Israel Defense Force; IDF; citizen army; U.S. Army

19. ABSTRACT (Continue on reverse if necessary and identify by block number)

The author of this report uses the IDF as a model in much the same way the U.S. Army has traditionally examined foreign armies. He describes the force and hones in on the significant aspects such as its force structure and mix, officer corps and equipment. Having examined the model he rejects what may not be transferrable and then lists what his examination has revealed as relevant to today's post-cold war U.S. Army. For each of the diverse yet relevant aspects, the author shows how one might superimpose them on U.S. ground forces and even touches on the significance of the Joint lessons the IDF offers.

20 DISTRIBUTION / AVAILABILITY OF ABSTRACT ☒ UNCLASSIFIED/UNLIMITED ☐ SAME AS RPT ☐ DTIC USERS	21 ABSTRACT SECURITY CLASSIFICATION UNCLASSIFIED	
22a. NAME OF RESPONSIBLE INDIVIDUAL Marianne P. Cowling	22b TELEPHONE (Include Area Code) (717) 245-3001	22c. OFFICE SYMBOL AWCI

DD Form 1473, JUN 86   Previous editions are obsolete.   SECURITY CLASSIFICATION OF THIS PAGE
UNCLASSIFIED

ECONOMY OF FORCE: A TOTAL ARMY, THE ISRAEL DEFENSE FORCE MODEL

Charles E. Heller

March 15, 1992

* * * * * *

The views expressed in this report are those of the author and do not necessarily reflect the official policy or position of the Department of the Army, the Department of Defense, or the U.S. Government. This report is approved for public release; distribution is unlimited.

* * * * * *

Comments pertaining to this report are invited and should be forwarded to: Director, Strategic Studies Institute, U.S. Army War College, Carlisle Barracks, PA 17013-5050. Comments also may be conveyed directly to the author by calling commercial (717) 245-3376 or DSN 242-3376.

* * * * * *

Accesion For	
NTIS CRA&I	☑
DTIC TAB	☐
Unannounced	☐
Justification	

By	
Distribution /	
Availability Codes	
Dist	Avail and / or Special
A-1	

FOREWORD

There are a number of "citizen" armies around the world, yet none receive so much attention as the Israel Defense Force (IDF) ground component. This spotlight not only reflects the intensity of the five wars it has fought in its 54 year history, but also its absolute reliance on its reserve forces and "hand me down" equipment.

The U.S. Army, over its 217 year history, has used other armies as models. During the War for Independence, the Continental Army copied Great Britain's forces. At the end of the Napoleonic wars, study of the French army was the accepted practice until the Franco-Prussian War, when the Prussian army became a model for the U.S. Army. After World War II it became in vogue to marvel at the German *Wehrmacht*, especially its campaigns in the East against the former Soviet Union.

The author of this report uses the IDF as a model in much the same way the U.S. Army has traditionally examined foreign armies. He describes the force and hones in on the significant aspects such as its force structure and mix, officer corps and equipment. Having examined the model he rejects what may not be transferrable and then lists what his examination has revealed as relevant to today's post-cold war U.S. Army. For each of the diverse yet relevant aspects, the author shows how one might superimpose them on U. S. ground forces and even touches on the significance of the Joint lessons the IDF offers.

With the increasing pressure on the defense budget and growing domestic problems such as drugs, crime and declining industrial base, it may be the time to use new models to break old paradigms.

KARL W. ROBINSON
Colonel, U.S. Army
Director, Strategic Studies Institute

BIOGRAPHICAL SKETCH
OF THE AUTHOR

COLONEL CHARLES E. HELLER is the U.S. Army Reserve Advisor to the Strategic Studies Institute, U.S. Army War College. A graduate of both the U.S. Army Command and General Staff College and the U.S. Army War College, he also holds a B.A. in history from Hofstra University and an M.A. and Ph.D. in U.S. history from the University of Massachusetts/Amherst. An Army Reserve Ordnance officer in the Active Guard/Reserve Program, his last assignment was as Chief, Mobilization Training Division, U.S. Army Reserve Personnel Center. He has served on active duty with the 8th Infantry Division in Germany. He is the author of a number of articles on military history and wrote a *Leavenworth Paper* on chemical warfare in World War I while on the faculty at the U.S. Army Command and General Staff College. He is also the coeditor of *America's First Battles* published by the University Press of Kansas.

PREFACE

The paper you are about to read was written as a result of a number of factors. The first was an intellectual curiosity about an armed force, the Israel Defense Force (IDF), that everyone mentions when discussing the Middle East and modern desert warfare, yet knows very little about when asked about its infrastructure and how it functions. One of the most intriguing characteristics is the reserve which comprises 82.6 percent of its total strength.[1] The second was the U.S. cold war victory which has brought about defense budget cuts that will become even deeper as the 21st century approaches. Lastly, its writing is influenced by the current downsizing of the post-war U.S. Army coupled with the first major reserve call-up since the announcement of the Total Force policy. Both of these events have resurfaced the debate about the proper mix of active and reserve forces.

After examining the IDF, its structure, force mix, weapons, officer corps, women's corps and missions, the conclusion reached is that some aspects of this force could serve as a model for the post-cold war U.S. Army. These aspects are:

- Acceptance and practice of a Total Army concept.
- Flow-through system (active to reserve service).
- Enlisted Service required prior to commissioning.
- National Service.
- Significant equipment modernization through modification.
- Peacetime missions that are domestic nation building in nature.
- Joint organizational structure of the IDF.
- Youthful senior officer leadership.

- Brigade as the basic building block of the Army's force structure.

The list is diverse, but all of the topics have varying degrees of relevancy for today's U.S. Army. The problem may not be the topics themselves, but as one Army War College faculty member remarked, "How do we get there from here?" That question probably can best be answered by the senior leadership of the Army, some of whom, like General Frederick M. Franks, Jr., Commander, Training and Doctrine Command, have already begun to lay the foundations.[2]

ECONOMY OF FORCE: A TOTAL ARMY, THE ISRAEL DEFENSE FORCE MODEL

Introduction.

In seeking to survive as a credible deterrent force in the wake of cold war demobilization, U.S. Army senior leaders may find in the Israel Defense Force (IDF), or *Tzava Haganah L'Yisrael*, a model of an army which has always operated in an economy of force environment. With this force Israel has rapidly mobilized and always won its wars. A significant reason for both economy of force and for success lies in its reserve. A reserve one might add, that has the capability to rapidly mobilize and, without post-mobilization training, achieve success in combat. The U.S. Army does not require activation of hardly any of its Reserve Components (RC) in the approximately 24 hours the IDF requires, but as the Active Component (AC) becomes smaller, it would seem to require an increase in the missions and mobilization readiness of its RC. Part of the solution to the U.S. Army's challenge of downsizing at the end of the cold war while retaining an adequate force to accomplish anticipated missions is a new approach to force structure and mix, manning and equipping, and peacetime missions by using selected aspects of the IDF model for the restructuring that needs to take place.

Unlike the U.S. RC, the citizen-soldiers of the IDF are not a "reserve," but very much a part of an integrated total force structure. Because of the integration, regular or Permanent Service (*Keva*) officers and noncommissioned officers (NCOs) know intimately their reserve forces (*Miluimm*) because they understand the IDF is a reserve army.[3] The IDF reserve soldier may or may not be issued the latest equipment available. But regardless, many *Miluimm* units enter combat alongside *Keva* units. The *Miluimm* soldier's number of days on active duty varies a great deal because it depends on the political climate of the region. Yet the type of active duty does not necessarily equate to training in traditional combat skills because the service may be riot control in Gaza or patrolling the northern border. Even so, the amount of time required each year as a minimum by law in a peacetime environment, 45 days, is close to the 39 drill days of the U.S. Army's RC. Therefore, is it not possible for the U.S. Army's RC to shorten its post-mobilization training time and deploy as part of a contingency force?

The IDF has a number of peacetime missions that make it invaluable to the nation, so much so that if peace were to finally arrive in the Middle East, the IDF would continue to have the full support of the government and the people. From the early beginnings of the nation the IDF has been the vehicle to assimilate very diverse groups of immigrants from all over the globe. The IDF is also responsible for a paramilitary youth scouting organization, and even has a program to take youth gang leaders out of the slums to educate and train them with the expectation that they will return to their homes as positive role models. For the ultra-religious minority there are a host of alternative national service programs ranging from teaching in new towns to hospital work. The Army is also the national educational institution, not only training Israeli youth, but encouraging all ranks to pursue civilian educations, rewarding its soldiers with additional pay for university degrees. Finally, it has been instrumental in the construction of frontier settlements and other environmental projects such as reforestation.

In the Beginning.

In the history of modern warfare there has never been a citizen army that has mobilized as rapidly and fought as effectively as the IDF. The reason is obvious. Few countries in the world face the constant threat to their national security and are at such a geographic disadvantage as the state of Israel. The IDF is unique among the modern armies of the world because, unlike other armed forces, it has developed under the constant pressure of a state of war with its neighbors. Except for some British influence and Swiss force structure and mix adaptation, the IDF evolved on its own. Israel's armed forces created strategic and tactical doctrine as they evolved through one conflict and then another. From force structure and weapons systems to basic soldier skills, the Israelis have learned through trial and error what is necessary to survive on a modern battlefield. This evolution began in the 1948-49 War for Independence and has continued to the present. In 1949, when the armistice was signed ending Israel's first war, Chief of Staff Yigal Yadin and his staff were charged by then Prime Minister David Ben Gurion with the task of building a defense establishment capable of providing the means of survival against overwhelming odds. The parameters were clearly defined by a society many of whose members had learned by oppression to distrust standing armies, an economy that would never be able to afford the size armed forces necessary to absolutely guarantee national survival, and a small population from which to draw its manpower. One European nation's armed forces, Switzerland, appeared to fit the new government's requirements.

Yadin and other members of the new IDF spent several months in Switzerland studying that country's citizen army. It became apparent that this tiny nation's armed forces could serve as a model to suit Israel's security needs. The Swiss Army, they found, was composed of a small cadre of regular forces primarily responsible for training, long-range planning, and maintenance of a "massive civilian army supported by large qualities (sic) of armor, artillery, air force, etc." Active service in the Army was mandatory and so was reserve duty.[4] For Israeli purposes the Swiss model required some adaptation, but it was a workable solution for a country whose cultural past, population size, and small economy would not tolerate a large standing army. Yadin proposed a small Permanent Service (*Keva*) cadre of primarily officers and NCOs; a Compulsory Service (*Hova*), called National Service by many Israelis, composed of conscripts, both men and women; and a large body of immediately available reserve units and individuals (*Miluimm*) that would include all soldiers who had completed their initial service obligation.

The nation's leadership included, in addition to national security, another mission which looms in importance and justifies the force even in peacetime. This second mission is "national development," that is molding successive waves of immigrants into citizens of the state, most recently the massive immigration of Jews from the former Soviet Union. Prime Minister Ben Gurion, when in office, described the IDF role as a "formidable part in integrating the different immigrant groups . . . ." into the society and as a ". . . great instrument for education . . . ." Even if the Middle East was at peace, Israel would "still continue to depend on the dynamic represented today by the IDF to fulfill a vast assignment of national development."[5]

The Organization of the IDF.

Prime Minister Ben Gurion approved the creation of a single General Staff (*Hamateh Haklali*) for all the armed services, Army, Air Force, and Navy. The results were, in some ways, similar to the U.S. Joint Staff (see Figure 1). The Army (*Zahal*) as the primary service, is commanded by the Chief of Staff (*Ra'Mat'Kal*), a Lieutenant General, who functions in a role like the U.S. Chairman of the Joint Chiefs in wartime. In peacetime the Navy (*Heyl Hayam*) and Air Force (*Heyl Havir*) are controlled by their respective commanders. In war these commanders are General Staff officers who report to the Chief of Staff. The General Staff currently has five branches, each commanded by a Major General: Operations, Quartermaster (Logistics), Manpower (Personnel), Intelligence, and Planning.

The Operations Branch is commanded by the Deputy Chief of Staff, who also is responsible for Research and Development, Training and Doctrine and the Senior Service School. The Manpower (Personnel) Branch is currently divided into six separate commands: Personnel Automated Data Processing Systems, Civil Engineers, Military Police, Civilian Education, and Youth Scouting or *GADNA* (a Hebrew acronym for Youth Battalions, but more commonly called "Bow and Arrow" for its insignia). The Women's Corps, *Heyl Nashim* or *CHEN* (Charm in English) is commanded by a female brigadier general. The Intelligence Branch, although commanded by combat arms Major General who is rotated in and out of the position, has a staff headed by a permanent career intelligence officer. The Quartermaster, or Logistic Branch, controls two

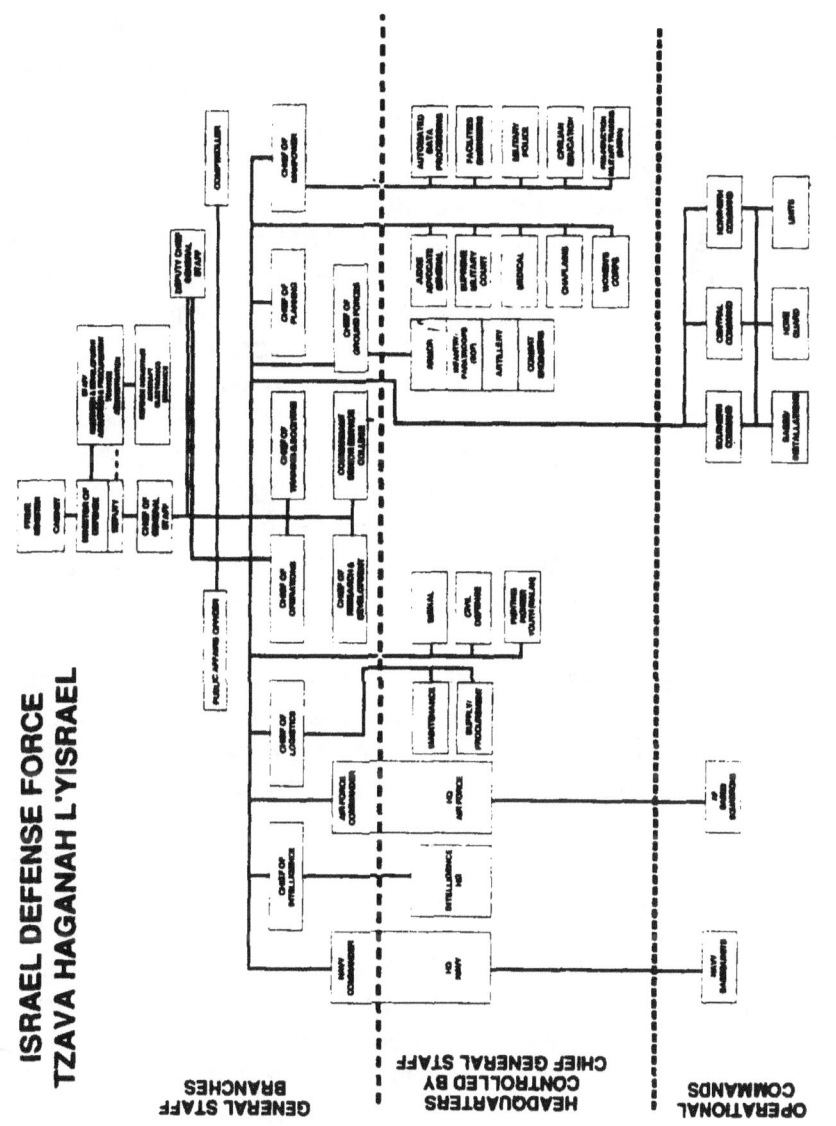

Figure 1.

subordinate sections, Maintenance and Supply. The Planning Branch conducts strategic, long-range planning.

Also reporting directly to the Chief of Staff are a number of Commands: Communications Command, Civil Defense, the *NAHAL* or Fighting Pioneer Youth (*Noar Halutz Lochaim*), and the Ground Forces Command, a training, and tactical doctrine command with the following subordinate commands: Armor, Infantry and Paratroops (to include Commandos or what the United States would now call Special Operations Forces), Artillery, and Combat Engineers (Engineers are also responsible for chemical warfare as they were initially in the U.S. World War I army). These subordinate Ground Force commands organize and train individuals prior to their deployment to one of the territorial commands. They also have a strong say in weapons development and procurement. The *NAHAL,* an organization that is reminiscent of the early American frontier militia system, provides a combination of military and agricultural training for youth who maintain settlement security while farming the land. Soldiers in *NAHAL* are also used as a mechanized infantry brigade reinforcement pool to the territorial commands. In addition to these organizations, five functional commands report directly to the Chief of Staff: Judge Advocate General, Supreme Military Court, Medical, Women's Corps, and Chaplains.

Israel is divided into three IDF territorial commands, Northern, Central, and Southern. Their commanders report directly to the Chief of Staff and they function in some ways similar to the U.S. regional Commanders-in-Chief (CINC). These commands provide the administrative and operational framework for the IDF. Each has a Major General commanding and deputy staff officers responsible for operations, training, and supply. Within the boundaries of each territorial command, both *Miluimm* and *Keva* officers command divisions and brigades. The territorial commanders are specifically responsible for the defense organization of that particular geographic area including the administration, training and mobilization of the reserve forces. An important aspect, and one that reflects the total force nature of the IDF, is that *Miluimm* and *Keva* units (with *Hova* personnel) and soldiers of all ranks are intermixed and interchangeable within each command.[6]

An Integrated Force.

Given this force structure, the most critical and unique aspect of the IDF is the *Miluimm*, which is "its most important operational component rather than just being an appendage to the regular force." Driven by economy of resources in dollars and manpower, the IDF developed an immediately deployable reserve which today comprises 82.6 percent (494,000) of its total military strength of 598,000. The regular force numbers 104,000, of which 88,000 are compulsory service soldiers. These are stunning figures and percentages when one considers the threat and the small margin between victory or defeat for a nation the size of New Jersey.[7]

No other modern army can duplicate the factors that influence and mold the IDF. Certainly culturally, politically, economically, and geographically the country has little in common with America except for being a democracy and sharing many Western cultural traits. Also, the imminent possibility and nearness of the threat posed by the likes of brutal dictators Saddam Hussein and Hafez al-Asad have never been duplicated in the Western hemisphere. However, some elements in the nature of the IDF may provide a U.S. peacetime army facing significant troop reductions and budget cuts, ideas to improve the mobilization and combat readiness of its Total Army force structure, keep its technological edge, maintain end strength, and become an decisive force in revitalizing the society it serves.

The IDF, as an institution, has a very positive attitude toward its reserve. Obviously, with the bulk of the force being citizen-soldiers, the emphasis has to be there. Part of the IDF emphasis is the reliance on the integration of its components to mold an affordable deterrent force. The IDF's mix of *Keva*, *Hova*, and *Miluimm* individuals and units within the force structure is a major ingredient for the success of the force in combat. The assignment of *Keva* soldiers to reserve units is accepted as the norm and does not affect career progression or signal a terminal assignment as is many times the case in the U.S. Army. In fact the IDF *Keva* officer's assignment to reserve units may even enhance advancement. *Keva* officers can be assigned down to battalion level in staff positions in reserve units. This cadre appears to be placed in IDF reserve units with no particular motive other than finding the best officer for the assignment. The element of stability, experience, and knowledge of full time manning personnel is one factor that influences battlefield results for *Miluimm* units. However, *Miluimm* officers who show promise can and do command at brigade and division level as well as serve in staff positions and offices throughout the *Keva*.

Hova, the IDF Manpower Pool.

Since national survival depends on the IDF, military service is a significant part of the life of an Israeli. As a consequence, there is an effort to prepare young people for their eventual national service. A majority of Israeli boys and girls at the age of 14 join the *GADNA*, a paramilitary organization. Early in its history the emphasis of this organization was on small arms training; today it is on physical fitness and sports. However, the purpose is not so much military training, but rather, in addition to physical fitness and outdoor living, it instills in youth a knowledge of the nature of the nation's "special security situation." In one sense, it is citizenship education to an extreme degree bordering on indoctrination, preparing youth to face Israel's political realities and giving meaning to service in the *Hova*.[8]

The IDF's manpower pool for the *Keva* and *Miluimm* is the *Hova*, compulsory or national service. From these ranks flow men and women into the *Keva* and *Miluimm*. Every Israeli citizen is required to perform military service or an alternative. A nationwide announcement is made every month by birth date for those youth who have reached their 18th birthday. About 92 percent of all males and 60 percent of all females are inducted. The lower percentage for women can be attributed to the exemptions offered: marriage or engagement, religion, and less than 8 years of formal schooling.[9] In addition, the mental and physical standards are higher for females than for their male counterparts. Standard exemptions for religion, conscientious objections, or physical disabilities are given to males although the latter must be extreme and many young people with handicaps still serve in the public sector. One of the most commonly used exemptions is for religion. A very large number of young men of military age are ultra-orthodox Jews attending *Yeshiva* (religious school). This exemption is a source of contention among secular Jews and is a serious weakness in sharing the military burden in National Service. Non-Jewish citizens, Druze, Christians, and Circassians also have a service obligation. Israeli Arabs are exempted. A small number of Bedouin and Christian Arabs volunteer for military service. The standard service is 3 years for men and 20 months for females. There are nonmilitary options for religious women who wish to serve and there are also special arrangements for those youth attending *Yeshiva*. The *Yeshiva* youth are offered a 5-year enlistment which allows school attendance during military service. Open to high school graduates, the inductees are given a 1-year deferment and enrolled in one of 15 special religious schools called "*yeshivot hesder*." The youth serve two 1-year periods in the army and two 1-year periods at their studies. When their *Hova* service is completed, they finish their reserve service with no special privileges.[10]

The new *Hova* recruits are all sent to *Ba'K'UM*, the Hebrew acronym for the "Absorption and Assortment Base." Prior to arrival, while still civilians, all conscripts have undergone their initial extensive medical and psychiatric examinations, and batteries of intelligence and aptitude testing. Level of civilian education, Hebrew language ability and personal preferences are also considered. Conscripts are then separated into 14 classifications. However, a review of all the human factors will continue until the new soldier is settled in his or her unit.

Basic training in the IDF is required of everyone, even those earmarked for the Navy or Air Force. The training has so many different tracks that it appears to an outsider that it is tailored to each individual who enters the IDF. The only exemptions for some parts of the demanding combat training under extremely harsh conditions are given to those individuals with very low physical or mental standards. These conscripts will be allowed to take less demanding and short duration courses prior to being assigned to noncombat specialties. Training dropouts are recycled until they complete the course assigned. There is no waste of any resources, especially human.

Very little time in any of the training schedules is devoted to drill and ceremony. The emphasis is on combat survival skills with large blocks of instruction given to weapons qualification and physical fitness. The IDF conducts much of its training in the field and with live fire whenever possible. The purpose of making training as realistic as possible is because the vast majority of recruits will enter the *Miluimm*. The IDF, therefore, needs to make the citizen-soldiers' transition from peace to war less traumatic so that they will immediately adjust to the noise and confusion of battle. As for military discipline, it is based on a philosophy of "group consciousness" what Yigal Allon called "internal":

> The education for discipline should be oriented towards the activation of conscious and good will. The more the fighter will identify with the mission of the army as a whole and the task of his unit in particular, the stronger and more sincere his discipline will be ... The importance of the formal framework [of discipline] should not be dismissed, but woe to the army which has to rely on this exclusively.[11]

Inductees, if qualified, have the opportunity to select specialties. A number of special qualification jobs exist in the Intelligence corps. Many recruits attempt to join elite units like the paratroops. Any of these voluntary career options extend the *Hova* service obligation because of the additional training and the cost of the investment in that individual. Officer candidacy, for example, requires one additional year of active service. Those who wish to volunteer for elite units or officer training can only do so if they are in the upper six levels on the classification scale.

The Officer Corps.

No individual can become an officer in the IDF without having trained and served in the *Hova* as an enlisted soldier. There are no military academies; their creation would have been unacceptable for the "egalitarian ethos of Israeli life" for such schooling has "connotations of social inequality."[12] However, as modern war and weapons became more sophisticated there was a need to increase the number of college educated officers, especially in the technical branches (in the U.S. Army, Combat Service Support [CSS]). As a consequence an Academic Reserve Program was created.

This program for officer candidates is similar to the Reserve Officer Training Corps in the United States. A deferment is granted for enrollees who continue their university educations. They train during their summer vacations as recruits in basic training and then Squad Commanders' course. After these courses they receive additional officer orientation training and military schooling which emphasize their specialty. The objective of the program is to specifically increase the number of college educated professionals, for example, doctors, attorneys, lawyers, and engineers in the *Keva* and *Miluimm*. Upon completion, their total obligation on active duty is extended to 5 years. Unlike the U.S. Army policy, as is the case for medical doctors for example, these specialists are not promoted with minimum time in grade. In fact, the privilege of below the zone promotions is reserved exclusively for combat arms officers.[13]

The only other source of commissioning in the IDF is through the ranks by a careful screening of *Hova* soldiers that begins at induction. Each soldier is subjected to extensive batteries of tests to determine his or her talents and leadership qualities. Those with the highest motivation and intelligence are usually placed in combat units and programmed for leadership training in all branches of the service. After basic training, those *Hova* soldiers who by testing, observation, motivation, and desire indicate officer potential are selected for further training. They enter a rigorous program with no guarantee of a commission. There is additional schooling in the branch of service, decided again by batteries of tests, interviews, personal preferences, and needs of the IDF. In a reversal of U.S. Army training schedules in general, those *Hova* soldiers selected for the combat arms have a lengthier basic training period than those destined for noncombat arms specialties. Those potential officer candidates selected for the CSS branches attend schooling in their specialty while their combat arms counterparts are sent directly to units which become their parent unit of assignment (an association similar, in practice, to the defunct U.S. Regimental System). After 5 months all soldiers are evaluated for leadership potential. This evaluation also includes test scores from their initial screening. About 50 percent pass on to the Junior Commanders' Courses (NCOs) in their respective branches. The courses are rigorous and stressful, and are conducted primarily under field conditions. Interestingly, many instructors are *Hova* soldiers themselves, many of whom are female, and not *Keva*. Aside from field training and rotation of command positions, the junior commanders attend classroom seminars to learn about the psychological elements of leadership and command.[14]

From the ranks of the junior commanders, the final selection for officer candidates is made after even more evaluation. Those who fall by the wayside remain in leadership positions as NCOs. The survivors who become officers reap the benefits from the 2 years or so of enlisted training and experience. This means that later officer training can be focused more on cognitive skills resolving both tactical and leadership problems than on individual basic combat survival skills. Most of the course is conducted in the field and much of it appears similar to the rotation of command responsibility during U.S. Ranger training to develop problem solving and leadership skills. What appears significant is the reliance on a "follow me" type of leadership to an extreme degree. Thus "knowing that he will be able to 'pull' his men after him by being the first to advance, the officer can choose daring tactical solutions which he might otherwise have had to reject." The goal is to instill in the officer intellectual and leadership skills to motivate reluctant soldiers in combat by personal example. This has always been the idealized goal of the IDF from its very beginning.[15]

In an army that is primarily officer led with NCOs playing a secondary role in day-to-day administration and combat, it is interesting to note that the total officer corps is less than 10 percent of the IDF and in combat units only 6 percent. The IDF sees "regular service primarily as preparation for the extended reserve service...." However, the cadre nature of this reserve army is reflected in the higher number, 14 percent, of officers in the *Keva*.[16]

Perhaps the single most identifiable feature of the IDF officer corps is the youthfulness of its officers, primarily in the *Keva*. As it became a more professional army after 1967, some attention was given to how to maintain innovative, vigorous, and aggressive leadership. One solution was to grant leave to officers so they could obtain university degrees during their service and not prior to commissioning so that the intellectual stimulation of nonmilitary subjects would generate new thinking upon their return to duty. While many armies bemoan the loss of competent, experienced leaders, the IDF believes that a constant turnover brings new thoughts and a greater willingness to try new concepts when focusing on problems and changing situations. Thus another solution for maintaining an open forum for new ideas was to retire its most senior, and therefore most successful officers early with half pay. It is not so much that new leadership always has new ideas, but that the IDF's "collective capacity to absorb rapid change without disruption derives from the open-mindedness of its young officer corps." In the IDF the senior officers propose innovative changes rather than being the group that traditionally takes a more conservative approach. British Army historian and theorist Major General J.F.C. Fuller, in his short monograph *Generalship, Its Diseases and their Cure*, would applaud the IDF's recognition of the inherent pitfalls of maintaining an older general officer corps.[17]

The *Keva*.

The Permanent Service, or *Keva*, the IDF's regulars, are only a small fraction of this reserve army. The *Keva* numbers about 16,000 officers and enlisted soldiers, but is composed primarily of the former. This end strength is the same as the U.S. Regular Army out of a force totaling 8 million in 1945. Its members do not relate to the term careerism given to the U.S. Active Component. Rather, the officers and NCOs see themselves as being motivated primarily by a desire to serve the nation. Currently, many are drawn to the regular establishment by such things as "its importance, the inherent authority, and the challenge" and not by factors such as promotion and benefits, even though those are significant. For example, *Keva* officers' pay scale is one of the highest in the nation and the fringe benefits extensive. Yet, on the other hand, the family living conditions, separation, constant danger and the individual's feeling of personal responsibility for national survival are a heavy burden. For officers especially, the time consumed by their jobs even in peacetime is significant and expected as the norm. However, there is a saying in the IDF about office lights burning all night giving the impression of working late, but without anything being accomplished, a practice that can be likened to a U.S. Army tradition.[18]

Once a new soldier arrives at a *Keva* unit, yet another screening, as intensive as the entrance evaluation, takes place. Army psychologists are assigned to each unit. They help commanders assign individuals to specialties within the unit and also with the mix of personalities to make up efficient subordinate units. The IDF found, for example, that units composed of exclusively "high achievers" do not necessarily guarantee a more dynamic organization. As a direct result, the goal is to bring together a diverse group to form a section, squad or platoon. The psychologists also oversee peer evaluations. Questionnaires are given to soldiers asking them who in their unit would make a good squad or section leader. Likewise, NCOs are asked which one among them would make a good officer.[19]

Like the United Negro College Fund slogan, "A mind is a terrible thing to waste," the IDF makes every attempt to gain the maximum potential from every soldier. In most armies undereducated inductees or those lacking basic skills are placed in menial specialties. This is not so in the IDF. These soldiers are singled out in order to "raise their performance levels and capabilities through education." At a minimum, no soldier is released from *Hova* service until they have at least obtained an elementary school education. This insures that the society will maintain an educated work force pool.[20]

While the decision to remain on active duty is left to the individual, many receive strong encouragement from their commanders. The process is very selective and, as a consequence, there is a constant shortage of officers and NCOs. One analysis has noted that in the aftermath of the controversial war in Lebanon, some concern was raised within the IDF "that not necessarily the cream of the crop has chosen to remain on active duty." Those that turn down the opportunity to serve in the *Keva*, however, cite most often the "enormous stress" they have already experienced in training and the unwillingness to expose themselves to such a demanding career, and not political reasons.[21]

Implicit in a career in the *Keva* is the acceptance of the mission to insure the combat readiness of the reserve. This mission includes providing the support structure for the *Hova* and *Miluimm*. The *Keva*, like the U.S. Army AC, is responsible for long-range planning, training and preparation for combat, research and development, and the distribution and maintenance of all materiel. In addition to senior and key operational command positions, all installations and service schools are commanded by *Keva* officers. Also the *Keva* contains a great many officer and NCO technical specialists. Since much reserve unit equipment is becoming more sophisticated and must be ready at a moment's notice, there is a significant need for full-time personnel to provide constant maintenance, repair and supply stockage. Then too, many active duty personnel man the research and development agencies as well as staff positions for planning and all the other functions that need full time attention in any army.

The *Miluimm*.

An estimated 90 percent of all officers leave the *Hova* at the end of their required additional 12 months and are assigned to *Miluimm* units. Because there are *Keva* junior officer shortages, mainly due to the extremely high standards that are not waived under any circumstance, many of these Permanent Service officers do not have the opportunity to attend the Company Commanders' Course. As a result, the vast majority of officers in attendance are *Miluimm*. While training and education continues for *Miluimm* officers, promotions are slower and, as in any small armed forces, few rise above the rank of major. It is not, therefore, both a patriotic and second career as in the U.S. RC, but rather an obligation required by citizenship. Beyond service in a unit, some *Miluimnicks* (reservists) are also part of the IDF pretrained individual manpower pool. As the U.S Army has on occasion, for example, placed U.S. Army Reserve (USAR) Civil Affairs soldiers on Temporary Tours of Active Duty (TTAD) for OPERATIONS URGENT FURY and JUST CAUSE, the IDF will ask for volunteers in specific areas to return to active duty. The IDF also has individual reservists assigned to headquarters and a variety of other organizations who are similar to those who serve in the USAR's Individual Mobilization Augmentation (IMA) program. All of these assignments are coordinated by a very sophisticated single personnel command system that tracks and maintains the records of all individuals, *Hova*, *Keva*, and *Miluimm*, serving in the IDF.[22]

Since continued service in the reserve is so much an integral part of the nation's defense, the 11 months between *Hova* and the *Miluimm* is jokingly called "leave." In the *Miluimm*, men are eligible for mobilization until age 55 and childless women until age 34 although the latter are rarely, if ever, called to active duty. Each reservist is liable by law to be called up for 45 days annually plus time for other training. This additional time is usually one day a month or 3 days every 3 months for enlisted soldiers or 7 days for officers at the discretion of the local brigade commander. This duty may be to relieve a *Keva* unit or familiarize with a new weapon. At the age of 39 for men and 29 for women, the annual requirement is dropped to 14 days a year for enlisted soldiers while officers and noncommissioned officers can serve an additional 21 days per year. The Minister of Defense has broad discretionary powers to call reservists to active duty for longer periods than stated. However, *Miluimnicks* do on occasion remind the Minister, through letters, that since a state of war does not exist, their requirement to remain on active duty is not essential for national survival and, having served their required 45 days, they should be released from active duty. At age 45 *Miluimm* soldiers (officers are strongly encouraged) can join a local defense unit (*Haganah Merchavit*). Combat unit membership is restricted to enlisted soldiers under the age of 45 although many, in times of crisis, will voluntarily rejoin their old units.[23]

Reservists are usually assigned to a unit near their homes in a position to match their military occupational skill. The IDF, through its automated, centralized personnel system, exercises close watch over military skills. If a soldier has a civilian skill that matches a military specialty, the individual is certain to be placed in that specialty when conscripted. If it is likely a certain specialty will be "under strength" in the *Miluimm*, the IDF will "over strength" it in the active force. The Israelis believe that it is not efficient to change a soldier's specialty once he has acquired the skills on active duty. There are exceptions, but in practice soldiers maintain their initial specialties throughout their service.[24]

According to the International Institute for Strategic Studies, the *Miluimm* not only provides most of the total IDF end strength, but "the reserve corps forms the bulk of the combat forces of the IDF." According to the Institute's estimates, approximately 65 percent of the IDF's combat units are in the *Miluimm*. This can be compared to slightly over 50 percent combat units in the U.S. Army's RC. Armor, Artillery and special units are concentrated in only a few locations and necessitate some commuting for training days and mobilization. Each unit has its own armory. Training might be conducted at the armory or at special training centers. Other periods of active duty may find the *Miluimm* unit relieving a *Keva* unit on border patrol or performing internal security patrols or familiarizing on a new weapon. Unlike the Swiss system, *Miluimm* soldiers do not keep their personal weapons at home. Unit equipment is never switched between individuals or crews who perform their own maintenance when training. Since many armories are local, the *Miluimnicks* live in the same neighborhood and know one another. There is an obvious civilian tone to the *Miluimm* units and a familiarity not common within the *Keva*. However, officers at all levels, and all components, know their men personally.[25]

Miluimm soldiers are mobilized in one of three ways. Annual training periods are announced by mail with a 6 week advance notice. For emergency mobilization notification, the radio, press, and movie theaters are used; each unit has a special call sign. Unit commanders, who are notified by higher headquarters by messenger or telephone, activate teams of soldiers who speed through neighborhoods with alert rosters until the lowest private is notified. As noted previously, armor, artillery, and special or elite unit members are not concentrated in one geographic area and their notification is more difficult. Soldiers, upon receiving notification, report to their units and draw equipment. Some *Miluimm* unit mobilizations can take place as quickly as 24 hours. Mobilization is one aspect of the IDF's planning that has always worked, even in the confusion of the 1973 Yom Kippur War.[26]

Unlike the volunteer U.S. Army Selected Reservists, those immediately available for a presidential call-up, the *Miluimnick* is only paid what amounts to "pocket money." By continuously amended legislation, the Defense Service Law, a reservist receives full wages from his employer. The government compensates self-employed reservists. There is no retirement pay. Although the number of active duty days for training has varied over the years, the most recent being 35 days for enlisted and 42 days for officers until the age of 35, reserve duty can total as many as 60 days a year excluding periods of war.[27]

The *Miluimm* unit serves as an extended family and also takes on the characteristics of a traditional regimental system. In other words one might spend an entire military service in one brigade among people the soldier has known for the entire period of service, since there is an effort to assign *Miluimnicks* to units near their homes. This reduces mobilization time, makes these units extremely cohesive, and also breaks down the formality of military service. Officers, even senior in rank, are known by their first names and there is little saluting. Then too, employers in civilian life may be commanded by one of their employees. However, the relaxed nature of the relationships in no way detracts from the combat readiness of the reserve units.

Even though the IDF is predominantly a reserve establishment, most of its senior officers are in the *Keva*. Most, but not all, division commanders are *Keva* while the staffs are integrated with *Miluimm* and *Keva* personnel. Brigade commands within a division are mixed and their staffs integrated. The "rule of thumb," however, is that "reserve officers command reserve units." As in the U.S. RC, *Miluimm* officers, especially battalion and brigade commanders and their staffs, spend additional hours of their civilian time performing military duties. While many hours are spent at the unit armory or checking subordinate unit training or dealing with higher headquarters, the bulk of the time is usually spent dealing with individual soldiers' problems. The use of *Keva* as cadre in *Miluimm* formations seems to be the norm; however, their role appears administrative, training and maintenance oriented, allowing the *Miluimm* to make good use of training time.[28]

To support the *Miluimm*, there are a number of programs. Some service school instructors are also assigned as cadre to *Miluimm* formations. These soldiers link up with their reserve unit during training periods. Other *Keva* and *Hova* personnel are responsible for administration within the *Miluimm*. For example, a *Miluimm* brigade has a *Keva* liaison officer who, with a small staff, functions as a personnel manager and maintains contacts with the unit's citizen-soldiers. The liaison officer has a direct line to the battalion commanders and also has counterparts in brigade subordinate units. One of this officer's and the battalion counterpart's most important tasks is as "address-hunting operator[s]." Teams of soldiers regularly hunt through neighborhoods verifying the addresses and phone numbers of unit members. This must be done by face-to-face contact to guarantee the validity of alert roster information. In a way, this procedure is similar to the functions of the Individual Ready Reserve (IRR) Screening program mandated by the U.S. Congress for the U.S. armed services. These teams are also used for clandestine mobilizations.[29] The mobilization of *Keva* personnel with the units they support is the implementation of the Active Guard/Reserve concept in the U.S. Army. The full time manning personnels' expertise is of value in combat and adds to the efficiency of the unit. To relieve the administrative burden on units, each *Miluimm* brigade has a cadre of *Keva* and *Hova* soldiers for day-to-day operations.[30]

Women in the IDF.

The issue of women in the armed forces of the United States was once again brought to the fore during OPERATION DESERT STORM. The problem of limited manpower pool has always faced the IDF and became more pronounced when the army was expanded as a consequence of the 1973 war. The manpower problem is expected to become more pronounced in the U.S. Army as the number of military age males falls in the near term. As a consequence, it is useful to briefly explore the role of women in the IDF. Also IDF women are more involved in peacetime missions than their male counterparts in the *Hova*.

As indicated earlier, women serve in the *Hova* for 20 months as compared to their male counterparts service of 3 years. Also their *Miluimm* obligation is limited and they are not normally found in *Miluimm* units. For this reason they have been barred from certain specialties since the train-up time for those jobs was not worth the return. Shortages of manpower have changed this and opened many areas once reserved for males, especially in the *Miluimm*. Female soldiers, unlike those in the U.S. Army, by Israeli law, do not go with their unit of assignment when it displaces from garrison to combat except for those in "certain sensitive positions."[31]

A number of women merely accept their 20 months and complete their required service. Another group that wants to serve Israel, but cannot do so in the military because of religious beliefs, performs a "nonmilitary" duty that benefits the society. These women, from Orthodox Jewish families, join what amounts to a "teacher corps." They are trained by the IDF as teacher aids. Their assignments are to the families of working class school age children. These "soldiers" are responsible for seeing that the children understand and complete their significant load of school homework. Additionally, to handle the huge influx of Jews leaving the former Soviet Union, 500 female soldiers attended a crash 3 month course learning how to teach Hebrew to the new arrivals in "absorption centers."[32]

Those women who desire more than a teaching or secretarial position in the IDF undergo the same intense screening process as their male counterparts. A heavy concentration of women looking for more challenging assignments is in the area of training. According to the commander of *CHEN*, Brigadier General Hedva Almog, "if you were to tell Ground Forces Command to remove the great number of women instructors they have and return to using just men, they wouldn't be able to." For example, there is a highly trained group of female instructors at the Ground Forces Armor school. These women attend an instructor course learning to strip, assemble, and fire all organic weapons and pull maintenance on the tanks in the IDF inventory. In classrooms and on the ranges women instructors apply a firm hand, teaching basic trainees how to maintain and operate weapons and supporting systems found in IDF tanks, including the Merkava Mark III. Brigadier General Almog is also seeking positions filled by men for which women could qualify and fill. She discovered a very high turnover rate of operations officers in units deployed on the northern border. As a consequence she had the IDF send qualified women to a course for operations officers. This extended their service requirement for one year, but it eliminated the lack of continuity in operational planning along a very active border.[33]

IDF female officers face a problem similar to the U.S. Army in having limited senior positions for women. Only in the past few years have training options been expanded for women who wish to become officers. Now, in addition to the basic officers' course, there is the possibility of attending a course for female staff officers. However good the intentions of the leadership, they have yet to open additional positions in maneuver units for women. The current ratio for men advancing from major to lieutenant colonel is 1:1.5, yet for women it is 1:4. At the rank of lieutenant colonel, promotion to colonel is even more pronounced at 1:4 for men and 1:25 for women. As in the U.S. Army, those female officers in the "technological corps" stand a much better chance for promotion. This does not dampen the willingness to try to advance, and in "field units" there are 10 applicants for every available position.[34]

It appears that only in the *Miluimm* do women have an opportunity to enter nontraditional roles held by men in the *Keva*; hence the willingness of women to volunteer for the reserves even though, unlike their male counterparts, they rarely are called to serve beyond their *Hova* tour. Brigadier General Almog believes there are capable female officers who could assume a host of positions within combat units. The *Keva* usually insists, for example, that brigade adjutants (S-1) and logistics officers (S-4) should come through the ranks (combat command positions, etc.). However, some women have become *Miluimm* brigade adjutants and a rare few "assistant to a reserve divisional adjutant."[35]

Force Structure and Mix.

Although the specifics are classified, it may be possible to break down the force structure and mix by using a variety of open sources. The basic combat maneuver formation in the IDF is the brigade. There are three types of brigades: armor, infantry (several of the latter have dual capabilities i.e. mechanized and paratroop), and artillery. Divisions exist and are similar to any other nation's formations when conducting operations; however, in the IDF they are, in practice, brigade group headquarters. These headquarters function when an operation requires more than one brigade and the division is organized for the task at hand. Therefore, there are no permanently assigned brigades to a specific division. Three armored division equivalents are in the *Keva*. They contain two armor and one artillery brigade. Upon mobilization each is fleshed out with one mechanized infantry brigade. The *Miluimm* contains nine armored division equivalents composed of from two to three armored brigades. They also have one each artillery and mechanized infantry brigade. About 25 percent of the armor brigades are at full manning level and at least one, perhaps more, are at half strength and the balance are at cadre manning level. The *Keva* mechanized infantry is formed into five brigades. One brigade is trained as paratroopers, one provides troop support for the NCO school, and a third is the *NAHAL*. Of the mechanized infantry brigades, about half are manned at half strength and the balance are at cadre level. The one mechanized infantry division in the *Miluimm* has three airmobile/parachute brigades in an arrangement that appears somewhat similar to the now deactivated U.S. 8th Infantry Division (Mechanized) in the 1960s, when the 1st Brigade was composed of two mechanized battalions of the 509th Airborne Infantry. Two parachute brigades are at full complement, one at half and the balance, at least three, are at cadre level. There are three full-strength *Keva* artillery battalions (203mm M-110 Self-propelled) and one Lance battalion. According to recent news accounts, the IDF has at least 2 operational Patriot missile batteries at full strength. Most, but not all, of the artillery brigades, including those in the divisions, about 16 in all, are at cadre strength. There are ten cadre *Miluimm* regional infantry brigades assigned specific border sectors commanded by the three regional headquarters, North, Central, and South. Additionally, 2 Corps headquarters exist, but here too, as with the division headquarters in the force structure, they have no permanently assigned units.[36]

Because of the need to have equipment ready for immediate use and because of modern weapon sophistication, another cadre exists within each *Miluimm* unit; this cadre is formed by a number of *Keva* and *Hova* soldiers who are the day-to-day "maintenance, repair and supply specialists." The physical arrangements in which these full time personnel operate appear to be similar to the U.S. Army's Mobilization and Training Sites/Equipment Concentration Sites (MATES/ECS) and Area Maintenance Support Activities (AMSA). The most significant difference is that the *Keva* personnel mobilize and support a specific unit during wartime. The number of personnel available is unknown and it is difficult to even speculate at the level involved throughout the IDF. Israeli reserve soldiers take great pride in the fact that during any given inspection an officer can point to a vehicle and the operator can start it immediately. It is to the credit of this full time manning system that the Israelis in the 1973 Yom Kippur War had the ability "to have substantial elements of four reserve divisions fighting actively on both fronts within 30 hours of the surprise Arab offense and is proof of the general efficiency of the system, and of its overwhelming success in this instance."[37]

Equipment.

As with the success of the U.S. forces in the war with Iraq, much of the IDF's victories can be attributed to "modern" equipment. A number of unique aspects contribute to the equipping of Israel's armed forces. Again, the road taken by the IDF is based on the two constants that necessitate the need for a reserve army, tight funding and small manpower pool. In a sense, the Israelis have practiced New England thrift and made it a fine art. Old Yankees never throw anything away and everything in the IDF inventory is used and repaired until it cannot be used for its original purpose or any other. Why else would the IDF still have in its inventory, reported by the International Institute for Strategic Studies, 4,400 U.S. World War II M2/3 half track armored personnel carriers? As late as the 1973 War, the IDF was sending into battle World War II Super Shermans with modified 105mm guns.[38]

The IDF also fields 1,080 British Centurion World War II tanks that have been upgraded over the years. The most notable changes are a modern engine, an American automatic transmission and a 105mm gun. About 550 Korean War era U.S. M-48A5 are also in the IDF inventory. These have been so modified to actually be M-60s under the armor, the Israelis replacing the 90mm gun with a 105mm version, adding a fire control system and an air cooled diesel engine. Their inventory also includes both 1,000 M-60/A1 and 660 M-60A3s, all modified in some way including the use of reactive armor. But what especially indicates their cost-saving ingenuity is the placing into service of captured Soviet equipment including 488 T-54/55 (350 modified T-67 versions). These modifications include replacing the 100mm gun with a 105mm, a U.S. power train, air conditioning, fire control system (many with night vision devices) and Western European supplied machine guns. Only the World War II German *Wehrmacht* could equal the IDF in its ability to make effective use of captured weapons, potentially a maintenance and logistic nightmare.[39]

The Israelis have shown the same resourcefulness when it comes to artillery. In time for the 1973 Yom Kippur War, the Soltam Company placed a U.S. 155mm howitzer on a modified Sherman M-4A3E8 (World War II tank nicknamed "Easy Eight") chassis with a Cummins diesel engine. The result was the L-33, and about 100 currently are in service. Modified U.S. M-109s (M-109AL), about 550, carry a longer barrel increasing the range from 14,600 to 18,000 meters; redesigned elevation and traverse mechanisms and improved torsion bar suspension have also been added. Interior redesign enables the vehicle to carry a larger basic load of ammunition.[40]

Other weapon systems purchased or captured by the Israelis have also undergone modifications. In addition to the continual improvement of weapon systems, the IDF's research and development branch, in close cooperation with the defense industry, has spawned a number of weapons ranging from the versatile infantry weapon, the Galil, which is used as a rifle, submachine gun and squad light machine gun, to the radically designed and highly sophisticated Merkava main battle tank. The IDF's approach to defense by modification of weapons is complemented by practical engineering efforts to protect the lives of its small manpower pool. For this reason the Merkava became the first Main Battle Tank (MBT) with a front mounted engine and transmission for the purpose of giving added crew protection. There are about 660 Merkava Mark I/II/III MBTs in the IDF inventory. The Merkava Mark III mounts a 120mm gun with three machine guns and a 60mm mortar. It has rifle ports for the nine infantry men it can carry in addition to the crew. Its fire control system has a electronic computer, laser range finder, night vision system, and a stabilized vertical and horizontal line of sight. Additionally, the tank can operate in a chemical environment with its high over-pressure fighting compartment, central filter and crew air conditioning. The Merkava is a remarkable vehicle and an impressive example of a defense industry that has the vision and technical ability to modify a host of purchased and captured equipment while continuing to design and build new weapon systems on a shoestring budget.[41]

Observations.

The IDF force structure and mix are battle proven. The Israelis have shown that an army with over 80 percent of its total force in its reserve can be molded into an effective fighting force. The Israelis have made such a system work because of the unique political, economic and social pressures placed upon it by history and geography. Their Army's system conserves money, manpower, and time. While the United States will continue to have the luxury of more time to expand its armed forces in the face of a threat, reductions in the size of the Army and the new global environment dictate the need for such an integrated, cost conscious, cost effective force in the future.

It is absolutely essential for the reader to understand that, in general, the two nations, the United States and Israel, are vastly different and that their armies are, as well. However, as indicated previously, there is some value in considering what within the IDF would be useful for a post-cold war U.S. force. Critics of the IDF will say "yes, but look who they have fought." The Israelis have always fought outnumbered, and outgunned. What they possess and hold in common with U.S. forces in the Gulf is superior leadership and a high caliber soldier who serve within the framework of a democratic society's army.

The Parts of the Model That Will Not Fit the U.S. Army.

Obviously the IDF model cannot be superimposed on the U.S. Army. A number of aspects are not only unacceptable to the U.S. Army, but also to the society it represents. Yet, these elements do not detract from those concepts worthy of consideration. After all, this study's purpose is to find ways to build a U.S. deterrent force on decreasing budgets.

It is unlikely, given the current global situation, that the American public would accept peacetime military conscription. The All-Volunteer Total Army, AC and RC, in the public mind, is the only acceptable method to man the force. Even a clear threat like the fall of France in 1940 could not provide rousing support in Congress for a draft, as evidenced by the 1941 extension of the Conscription Act by only one vote.

Many American women could not tolerate the IDF's legal restrictions on placing females anywhere near "the front." Combat units may have *CHEN* soldiers assigned; however, they are not in combat arms specialties and, with rare exceptions, those assigned to combat units are left in garrison when the unit deploys. Their weapons are for self-defense.

The American public would never tolerate any "scouting" youth organization being administered by the armed forces as a paramilitary, political indoctrination program. The *GADNA* would not have a chance of acceptance in the United States.

The noncommissioned officer in the U.S. Army has always been the "backbone" of the force. The only exception was during the officer-lead Viet Nam era army, which, all participants would acknowledge, did not function well. Since that time the Army has begun to rebuild the NCO corps to restore it to its traditional level of responsibility. Neither culturally nor on a practical level is an officer-led army without significant NCO participation practical for the U.S. Army.

The Relevant Aspects of the IDF.

There are an number of relevant aspects of the IDF in the general areas of force structure/mix, manning, training, commissioning, peacetime missions, and industrial preparedness that should be examined by the U.S. Army. A critical comparison of these issues may broaden the range of options for enhancing the capability of the U.S. Army in a peacetime environment with dramatic funding and manpower constraints. These alternatives not only may provide for a combat ready downsized army, but also reveal the potential for significant cost savings throughout the Department of Defense. The following areas are not necessarily listed in order of importance, but should be considered:

- Acceptance and practice of a Total Army concept.
- Flow-through system (active to reserve service).
- Enlisted service required prior to commissioning.
- National Service.

- Significant equipment modernization through modification.
- Peacetime missions that are domestic nation building in nature.
- Joint organizational structure of the IDF.
- Youthful senior officer leadership.
- Brigade as the basic building block of the Army's force structure.

Within the context of this study, keeping in mind the differences that separate both societies, their national military strategies and their armed forces, the following narrative considers each of these areas.

Acceptance and Practice of a Total Army Concept. The IDF has never had the U.S. Army's misfortune to be cast aside after a war because the threat to Israel has remained constant. In fact, after the last major war in 1973, "peace" brought a significant expansion of the force. The cost to the small nation has been tremendous. No one could ever suggest that Israel could afford, both financially and in the lost civilian productivity of scarce manpower, a large standing army constantly mobilized for war. Even with U.S. materiel and financial support, this full time readiness state is not attainable.

The solution to the problem was to create an integrated force and, in so doing, an extremely effective combat ready reserve has resulted. Because standards are for one army and the army staff focuses on all aspects of a Total Army, the parts, soldiers and units are interchangeable in battle. The only difference that has to be taken into consideration between the active and reserve components is the matter of hours' difference between arrival times on the battlefield.

The problem for the U.S. Army is how to downsize yet remain a credible deterrent force. The IDF has solved this problem by becoming a reserve army. To compound the U.S. current problem is the box into which the Army is placed in by a citizen-soldier tradition and the specter of Viet Nam. General Creighton Abrams attempted to solve the dilemma during the demobilization following the war in Viet Nam. He accepted the budget reductions because there was no alternative, but he was very sure that he was not going to allow two things to happen: the progressive disappearance of divisions with no end in sight, and the potential for a lack of public support for a conflict that the Army might be sent to fight in the future. His answer was the 16 division AC structure and, especially, the "Total Force Policy." The planned integration of the RC with the AC solved his two concerns because the 16 divisions required the introduction of the RC roundout concept. These same elements are part of the IDF's strengths. First and foremost, it is a reserve army which solved the budgetary problems and, second, the use of reserves make it a "citizens'" army.

However, there are problems with the way reserve forces are perceived and utilized by the U.S. Army. Part of the problem is the way the AC perceives these part-time soldiers, compounded by a host of contributing factors such as the lack of experience with, and practical knowledge about, the RC among senior AC officers. There is also a lack of focus on the RC as part of the same army. There has always been a great deal of rhetoric about "One Army," but obviously there is enough friction between the components to indicate that substance has been lacking in the talk about integrating the three components.[42] Why, for example, is there not one standard for training? There are also reserve-unique problems. Can RC large combat formations, brigade and above, be successful in maneuver warfare without significant post-mobilization training? Can the U.S. Army National Guard ever subordinate its political self-interest to recognizing and correcting its internal weaknesses?

Part of the problem for the U.S. Army that is not shared by the IDF is having two reserves, a Federal reserve and a highly politicized National Guard or militia. The IDF has a Federal reserve, but no comparable National Guard. A Federal "home guard" does exist in Israel, but it has no equivalent force in the United States, not even the State Defense Forces of the Governors comes close. The creation of the Federal reserve, the Officer Reserve and Enlisted Reserve Corps, later consolidated into the Organized Reserve Corps (ORC) by the U.S. Army in 1908, was to overcome the weaknesses of the state militia. The problem that the pre-World War I regulars saw was the distraction caused by state missions, and the inability to enforce one standard across-the-board in training, equipment, and leadership in the militia. The original intent of the Founding Fathers was very clear in defining the role the militia was to play in national defense. The U.S. Constitution describes the militia as a force of last resort available to ". . . execute the laws of the Union, suppress Insurrection and repel Invasions."[43] Only after legislative changes that were not really finalized until the 1916 National Defense Act and changes in 1920 could the Guard be legally deployed beyond U.S. shores. In fact the entire National Guard was drafted in 1917 to meet the letter of the law. Still, Governors time and again have challenged the Federal control and use of their Guards by the Federal government in the courts as unconstitutional. In essence the militia is an 18th century creation, unwieldy in the 20th, and an anachronism in the 21st century.

The Federal reserve, the USAR, formally the ORC, is a 20th century force more suited to the 21st century than the militia. The USAR not only has units, it has the right units, CS and CSS to marry up with maneuver units of the AC. It has the currently suggested number of separate brigades to be used as roundout. Further, it has the added value of being the only source of pretrained individual manpower. It manages the recently acclaimed IRR (the ARNG does have an IRR but it is composed of individuals within each state in transition who are not centrally managed). The USAR also contains the Individual Mobilization Augmentee program and the Retiree Recall program, both of great value as pretrained manpower pools during OPERATIONS DESERT SHIELD/STORM. It is for its versatility that it lends itself to being part of a contingency ready Federal force.

The IDF model offers a Federal reserve that is held to the same standards as the regular force. Rather than trying to control what amounts to 54 (the number of National Guard Adjutants General) separate armies who answer to a second authority, it would be far easier in a downsized U.S. Army to restructure itself into a Federal army, AC and USAR, not only for contingency operations, but also for the continental United States (CONUS) force structure including the TDA (Table of Distribution and Allowances) Army. The ARNG could then revert to its intended Constitutional role as a force of last resort for reinforcement and reconstitution. This would certainly please the State Governors for there would be less interference with their Guard units performing state missions. The Guard leadership would be pleased because they then would be able to retain their combat units.

An example of a CONUS-based Federal army is to mold the Training and Doctrine Command (TRADOC) into a fully integrated command. Since a smaller army will require fewer recruits going through initial entry training (IET) and advanced individual training (AIT), why not turn all training over to the USAR Training Divisions who would then be rotated through the few remaining centers for their AT? This would not only save AC slots for combat units, but dollars as well, since not only are all new soldiers trained, but it is done at the same time mobilization training for USAR units is conducted. USAR Forces Schools could also be rotated into TRADOC schools to teach certain short duration Military Occupation Specialty courses. Other, more difficult and lengthy courses would continue to be taught by AC instructors. Since many IDF instructors are *Hova* and produce quality graduates at the armor school and other ground forces school, why can't the U.S. Army place greater reliance on its expansion-capable Federal reserve force and have it serve a dual role? Of course there would be AC soldiers at all levels as a full-time cadre for scheduling, continuity and the doctrine side of TRADOC, and as in the IDF, it would be, as it is now, primarily AC.

Flow-through System. The intended purpose of an IDF *Keva* is to mold and build a pretrained manpower pool of former regular army soldiers for a reserve of individuals and units. All soldiers entering the *Hova*, career or reserves, receive the same initial training, education and indoctrination administered by the *Keva*. Once the training is completed, it is reinforced by active duty with the *Keva*. This is a simple way to maintain initial entry standards for training and education. It also breaks down unfamiliarity between the active and reserve components.

While this practice has not always been possible in the U.S. Army because of the greater manpower requirements, it has been more applicable to the USAR than the ARNG, especially in post-war periods following World War I, World War II, Korea, and Viet Nam. A strong argument for a larger active force can be made by the benefits which accrue to the reserve by use of a flow-through system. This system is why the IDF's *Keva* formations appear to have an abundance of specialties that are over-strength. As indicated above, the reason is to insure that the bulk of the force, the *Miluimm*, is at full strength and that all positions are filled, to use a U.S. Army term, with Military Occupation Specialty Qualified soldiers who have practiced their skills while on active duty. This process also serves, especially for junior officers, as a weeding out process to insure a quality force as it is done to an extent in the IDF.

Enlisted Service Required Prior to Commissioning. The IDF uses this system for three basic reasons. The society is uncomfortable with a military that is separate and apart from the citizenry, hence there are no military academies. Secondly, the entire process allows the IDF to be extremely selective as to who becomes an officer. The third reason is that officer training is exactly that in the IDF rather than an attempt to teach basic soldier skills and leadership at the same time. Even the Academic Reserve candidates are required to train as enlisted personnel. As any corporate executive or professional will tell you, the best way to learn the business is from the ground up. The IDF NCO corps is not threatened by this advantage for it makes its job easier, allowing the corps to spend more time mentoring soldiers rather than breaking in a constant succession of unseasoned, inexperienced second lieutenants.

National Service. There is no doubt that Israelis consider service to the nation as a requirement of citizenship. As noted, almost every youth, male or female, serves in some capacity: those with religious restrictions, those with low intelligence test scores, and those without formal education. It can be best described as a give and take national service. Individuals in the *Hova* are required to take civilian education classes. The minimum standard is an elementary school education and no soldier is released from active duty unless that soldier has obtained a certificate of completion. This guarantees that the population maintains a high literacy rate which, in turn, insures an informed citizenry and a more productive work force. The IDF also provides vocational training in trades that have a military application. This training not only insures the army has soldiers with necessary skills, it also is a boon to the nation's employers.

In a study prepared for the U.S. Department of Labor, *Workforce 2000: Work and Workers For the 21st Century*, the trends for type of work and the workforce required are diametrically opposed. The trends indicate a increasingly poorer educated and trained workforce. Yet the greatest growth will be in jobs that require the "highest education and skill levels": professional, technical, and sales. In all but one category, service occupations, jobs will demand more than a median education level. In a declining military age population, blacks and hispanics are projected to increase as a percentage of that population, the very minority groups trapped in poverty and in under-funded, crime and drug ridden urban school districts. For the United States, with the forecast of such a workforce crisis, National Service would act as a safety net to catch those for whom the public school system has failed.[44]

The focus or first priority of the Israeli National Service model is military training and service. Since the IDF active force is a conscript force, Americans would reject the model hands down. However, with adaptation, the concept of National Service could have a strong appeal to the general population with additional features such as a new Civilian Conservation Corps (CCC). The program would be the responsibility of any number of existing Federal executive departments, perhaps Education, Labor, or Interior. Initially, it could be voluntary for both males and females. As with the CCC, the Army's role would be to administer the initial orientation phase, developing hygiene, physical fitness, literacy, citizenship education, confidence building, and leadership skills, and conducting testing and evaluation. At the end of the orientation the participants would move to camps administered by the Army, primarily former and active military installations. They could select one out of a number of programs to complete their 2-year service. Some examples could be tutoring and teaching especially in the Headstart or adult literacy programs. Others could work in communities removing trash, and constructing play grounds and urban parks. The criteria for these options is the one the California Conservation Corps uses: a nonprofit agency or community project that is needed but would not be completed because no public money is available. Communities or agencies pay for the materials and an hourly rate for labor. This makes the Corps partially self-funded. Labor unions have no problem with the arrangement because of the criteria. Members of the Corps can be mobilized by the Governor for natural disaster relief work like during the February 1992 flooding in California.[45]

The California model, like the IDF model, offers opportunities to learn a trade or obtain a high school equivalency diploma. Since California treats the enrollees as government employees, the youth are eligible for medical treatment. There are some youngsters who have yet, in their late teens, to see a doctor or dentist. The same preventive medical care given to members of the California program could apply to a Federal National Service program.

Those individuals who express an interest in military service and qualify both physically and mentally would enter the first available Initial Entry Training cycle of the armed service of their choice. This option would retain the current educational incentives available today. The program could then retain the voluntary nature and quality of the armed services. The individual would go on to complete his 2 years' active service with 6 years' service in the RC.

National Service could also become the vehicle for a melting pot for American immigrants. Learning the language of their adopted country will help the children of immigrants enter the mainstream of society, opening up greater opportunities for advancement when coupled with job training.

National Service in Israel is also citizenship education. Traditional values of American society such as those listed in the Bill of Rights can be instilled in youth to insure the perpetuation of a democracy in a multicultural society. The very nature of the program implies commitment and dedication to the nation. What better way to bring a diverse society together? The bonding of men who were drafted and served in the eight million man Army in World War II was a very cohesive element of society for decades. National Service would provide that same cohesive cement for a society which lacks the ties that once bound it together.

Significant Equipment Modernization Through Modification. While the U.S. Army and other services have always upgraded equipment and weapons with modifications, the intent was to see the equipment through to the next generation, which during the cold war was usually just around the corner. This is not the driving force behind the IDF's upgrades of equipment. The decision is a measure of the lengths to which the IDF goes to economize scarce defense dollars. One might add, this is the reason the Israelis have been so successful with their home grown defense industry. The prime example is the Merkava, designed and built to improve upon the MBTs captured or purchased, most of which were designed for primary service on the plains of Central Europe.

The point that can be made is that by thinking, researching, and developing ways to improve upon equipment in the inventory and then putting into production these modifications, the IDF keeps the industrial base warm. One of the greatest industrial mobilization problems facing the United States is keeping the small subcontractors, who are usually one of a kind, in business. Extensive modifications to existing equipment and weapons systems can accomplish this and also keep research and development active with future system designs.[46]

One of the most significant examples of the Israeli defense industry's "Yankee thrift" is a 155mm howitzer for a self-propelled artillery piece. The IDF first used the chassis of a World War II U.S. Sherman M4A3E8, the G.I.'s "Easy Eight," to mount a domestic 155mm howitzer barrel. An improved version of the 155mm howitzer, the M72, was developed several years later. However, this time it was designed within a self-contained turret that, with some modification, can be placed on almos. any contemporary MBT or an older U.S. M48 or British Centurion. This was further improved by developing a longer barrel which extended the range an additional 3,000 meters.[47]

One of the most striking examples of this "economy of force" is the over 4,000 World War II U.S. M2/3 half tracks still in the inventory, many of which were purchased from scrap yards all over Western Europe after the conflict. If it were not for the fact that these vehicles have seen service in every Middle East War and that the Israelis place such a high value on protection for their soldiers, one could dismiss the number as merely giving the illusion of strength. Not so. The IDF has needed a troop carrier for the local terrain and has not been able to replace these U.S. museum pieces because of tight defense budgets. Obviously a great degree of modification has been made and these upgrades have apparently been sufficient to meet the requirements of modern war 50 years after the vehicles were first used in combat. Now that's economy of force.

All of these modifications, one can be certain, have added to the technical expertise of the Israeli defense industry. Without having the specific details, one can also assume that these changes continued to be incorporated into the design and building of new weapons systems such as the Merkava Mark III. What this implies for a downsized, tight procurement budgeted U.S. Army is greater attention to how exactly equipment and weapons in the current inventory can be continuously upgraded for the foreseeable future. It also means that research and development must take into consideration the need to not only extend the longevity of materiel, but also allow the design to be such that enhancements can be added indefinitely. This will not completely solve the age old problem of wartime requirements for a rapid industrial surge and long-term industrial mobilization, but it would be of comfort to know that such planning is being conducted.

There is one other area of IDF mobilization which should be addressed. As with our Civilian Reserve Aircraft (CRAF) program, the IDF has available on mobilization all civilian aircraft. However, mobilization means all means of transportation. Reservists driving commercial vehicles report with them, from "low boys" to bakery trucks and buses. Camouflage "paint" for civilian vehicles is mud. While it is difficult to imagine under any circumstances short of invasion that this would be necessary in the United States, it appears that, as a cost saving measure, the Army should be more attuned to purchasing vehicles and other equipment off the shelf rather than the more expensive exclusive military specification requirements. Like the modernization modifications, civilian vehicles purchased for military use could be designed by their manufacturers for the addition of a military modification package.

Peacetime Missions That Are Domestic Nation Building. As Prime Minister Ben Gurion stated, even in peace the IDF has a place in the life of the nation.[48] In the United States the Army has historically always held a similar place, although recently the cold war era was a lengthy departure from that norm. Have current military leaders, who served only in this threat oriented era, become so focused upon warrior missions and exclusive readiness for warfighting that their vision cannot readily accept and actively seek other missions? The resistance to military involvement in the war on drugs is a case in point. However, in the history of this nation the Army has delivered the mail, mapped and explored the continent, acted as a telephone/telegraph company, forecast the weather, run youth camps, conducted paramilitary training for businessmen, built roads and railroads, fought forest fires, performed riot control, enforced Federal laws, guarded the national parks, and in fact done everything the nation expected it to do. West Point, for example, would not have survived to this day, had it not been for the fact that it was justified by the engineers it produced who entered civilian life and helped build the nation.[49]

National Service involvement is but one possibility for a peacetime Army. This program was addressed previously in this study. However, the importance of such a domestic program to the Army as well as the nation needs to be addressed in greater detail. The Army initially objected to being used to administer Roosevelt's New Deal program, the Civilian Conservation Corps (CCC). There was good reason to protest. The size of the peacetime army had grown so small, a little over 132,000 officers and men, that the manpower demands would literally bring all military training to a halt. The problem was eventually eased by calling to active duty, officers and NCOs of the Organized Reserve Corps. While the Regular Army administered the districts, for example, George C. Marshall commanded both Fort Screven, Georgia and the CCC District "F". The individual camps were run by junior officers and senior NCOs of the Organized Reserve Corps (ORC). The Infantry Branch acting chief wrote to Marshall expressing the general sentiments of the Regular officer corps:

> This work is onerous and probably distasteful to the Army as it is not exactly military work but I feel that it is the salvation of the Army. In fact, it is my opinion that the Army is the only Governmental agency that was able to handle this proposition. I have noticed a cessation of talk of reducing the Army by four thousand officers since we started in on the conservation work.[50]

While this may appear a digression from the issue of peacetime missions, it merely shows that the Army has 1) traditionally dragged its feet at accepting peacetime missions, 2) been expected to perform peacetime missions by the chief executive and members of Congress, 3) reaped unintentional benefits as in 1932 such as preserving end strength, exercising mobilization procedures, providing leadership training to reserve officers and NCOs, and indoctrinating a vast number of military age youth many of whom eventually served during World War II. Most importantly, the CCC took unemployed youth off the streets, gave them self-respect, put discipline and structure into their lives, taught them trades, provided limited educational opportunities, and gave them a sense of community. The government was going to expand the voluntary program at the end of the decade and only the threat of war in Europe brought its termination. Not only did the military benefit from the graduates who flowed into the ranks, but the eventual entrance into the workforce of many of these youth must have certainly assisted industrial mobilization at the beginning of World War II.

A new CCC is but one peacetime mission for the post-cold war Army. Taking a look at the IDF model there are an additional number of tasks that could be assumed by the Army, especially by the U.S. Army Reserve, without harming and in some cases enhancing, mobilization readiness. Army officers and NCOs are, by training and experience, teachers. They could be given "short tours" to teach in inner city schools and rural areas. Training and Doctrine Command CSS schools, for example the Ordnance Center and School, could work with private industry to train unemployed youth and retrain displaced defense industry workers and soldiers in a number of trades. Engineer units could be used for environmental clean-up, rehabilitation of homes and schools in blighted urban areas, destruction of abandoned buildings and construction of parks, playgrounds, and areas for cultivation on the cleared ground. Medical personnel could teach hygiene and prenatal care, inoculate children, and treat minor illnesses. Military police and combat arms soldiers could man drug rehabilitation, and youth first-term offenders "boot camps." USAR Training Division personnel are ideally suited to assist Federal, state, and local corrections officers in the establishment of rehabilitation "boot camps." With coordination, Reserve soldiers could become "big brothers and sisters" to youth offenders rather than a parole officer.

The list is endless. The barriers to the use of Federal military personnel in an all out attack on drug traffickers and dealers are man-made obstacles that could easily be removed by a supportive Congress. After all, the Posse Comitatus legislation was passed by Congress as part of the 1877 election compromise. Its passage, few recall, was to limit the Army's enforcement of the 14th and 15th Amendments and its protection of black Americans from physical intimidation in the former Confederacy.

Joint Structure of the IDF. As with institutional foot dragging when it comes to duties such as running the CCC or participation in the war on drugs, the Armed Forces steadily resisted the efforts making them work together under Joint doctrine. Again, it was Congress assisted by a minority of reform minded service members who finally forced the passage of legislation requiring the services to institute Joint reform. After the problems that have surfaced in every war and the fighting over limited dollars in peace, the new Joint responsibilities were a breath of fresh air. One can only imagine how much more difficult OPERATIONS DESERT SHIELD/DESERT STORM might have been without this much needed reform. Jointness must continue and expand. Think of the waste and duplication of effort that now acts as a strangle hold on keeping the defense establishment as a creditable deterrent force. Why can we not adopt the IDF model? There is not a single reason other than service rivalry that can be cited for the maintenance of the current layers and layers of bureaucratic staff and command structure for each of the services. The Chairman of the Joint Chiefs should be the only Chief of Staff/Chief of Naval Operations/ Marine Corps Commandant. For that matter, why have the size Marine Corps we have today with its own air force? The IDF obviously has no such force because it has no overseas mission or a large navy. But the fact remains, why have a large Marine Corps with little or no staying power unless supported by Army CS and CSS as has been the case since World War I?

The services have made tremendous strides in many areas of Joint doctrine such as logistics, transportation, and medical. However, the pressure on the defense budget will become more and more intense. The dollars saved in making the armed forces a true Joint force similar to the IDF would allow this nation, like the Israelis, to have a strong deterrent force on a smaller budget. The dollars saved can be used to man and equip the most modern armed forces in the world. This may have been the line of reason President George H. Bush was suggesting in August 1990, when he said:

> The United States would be ill-served by forces that represent nothing more than a scaled back or shrunken-down version of the ones we possess at present. If we simply pro-rate our reductions--cut equally across the board--we could easily end up with more than we need for contingencies that are no longer likely--and less than we must have to meet emerging challenges. What we need are not merely reductions--but restructuring.[51]

Youthful Senior Leadership. Although the average age of the senior leadership, full colonels and general officers, has increased since the IDFs formative years, retirement is the norm between 40 and 50. Lieutenant colonels are in their mid-to-late 30s and there are no general officers over the age of 50. Officers do not settle into desk jobs to become part of a bureaucracy. They rotate in and out of assignments much like the average U.S. Army officer; however, because the country is so small geographically, families have a tendency to stay put and the *Keva* officer commutes to his or her home. This really creates no problem since the hours on the job during the duty week allow no time for family anyway. The IDF assists in the commute because every field grade officer has a driver and no need of a personal vehicle. There is no established formula for retirement although Moshe Dayan, while chief of staff, introduced the concept of retirement early enough to have a full and productive civilian career. Most officers do not reach high rank, nor do they expect to, and most retire in their 30s.[52] As indicated previously in the section on officers, the IDF believes that a younger officer corps is more flexible and creative.

Historically, when the U.S. Army becomes a peacetime establishment, its tendency is to slow down promotions which means that the senior ranks have stagnated the system. The post-cold war Army should increase selectivity at all levels from commissioning through promotions. The IDF practice of no implied length of service should also be adopted. The notion of performing a service to the nation and then returning to civilian careers while still young enough to use the leadership skills to benefit the society should be encouraged. This would not only strengthen numerous areas in the society that are in sore need of talent such as public administration, corporate leadership, and government, but build an informed Army constituency among the general population. General George C. Marshall suggested this role for reservists in his War Department Circular 347 and stated such a constituency was absolutely necessary in peacetime.[53]

Brigade as the Basic Building Block of the Army's Combat Forces. When the Army substituted AC brigades for the ARNG roundout brigades during the Gulf War, it provided a dynamic example of the IDF force structure model. It showed that a contingency force can be successfully built by independent brigades. A smaller Army cannot have division size units tailored and marked for specific contingency operations because, in the new world order, uncertainty is the only certainty. The use of brigade building blocks for a contingency allows a regional commander-in-chief much greater flexibility in tailoring his force.

Also a CONUS-based force must be a deployable force whose component parts should be fairly self-sustaining, anticipating early deployment for a forced entry or entrance into combat immediately after arriving in country. Brigades, as exhibited by the past use of independent brigades and current U.S. Army force structure and doctrine, can fulfill that requirement.

In a peacetime army composed of brigades, division commanders and their staffs can concentrate on the wartime mission of command and control and the direct coordination of subordinate maneuver elements without acting as another bureaucratic layer for peacetime paperwork. Training of maneuver units works best at the National Training Center at the brigade level.

Conclusions.

For the U.S. Army to survive as a combat ready deterrent force in a peacetime environment of drastically constrained defense spending, new approaches must be taken to problems that have lingered over the past century. While the IDF model may seem extreme to some, it does offer a different perspective on the problems facing the U.S. Army today and that could continue into the 21st century.

The current statement by the U.S. Army's Chief of Staff, General Gordon Sullivan, "no more Task Force Smiths," in reference to the ill-trained, ill-equipped group of men from the 24th Division that were sent to Korea to halt the avalanche of North Korean invaders, can also imply a failure of senior officer leadership in the period 1945 to 1950. From the serving Chiefs of Staff down, many officers failed to grasp the changing nature of the threat. But worse than that, they failed to keep the Army combat ready. They did not protest the severe budget cuts and did not use their influence to fix what was possible with the resources and the authority they had available.[54]

The pre-Korean War officer corps needed closer attention from CINCs on down. A number of officers who served in World War II were kept in command because of their past records with no attention given to their lack of potential in future wars. Some, unfortunately, were suffering the psychological effects of long confinement in prisoner of war camps. A few had medical profiles and still more were just not physically fit. There were those who had served beyond their usefulness and by any measure were well beyond their prime.[55]

Officer training and education were allowed to deteriorate. Training of young soldiers was not rigorous. The senior leadership seemed to have given up to those in the defense establishment who claimed that modern war with nuclear weapons did not require foot soldiers. The plans which Chief of Staff George C. Marshall had for the RC, integration, greater missions, etc. were never forcefully pushed and instead they were left to languish. Why didn't the senior leaders of the U.S. Army sound the alarm? What makes our officer corps at times neglectful of its past, blind to past lessons and unrealistic when looking to the future?

It is all too clear that if some new innovative thinking about the U.S. Army surviving in a peacetime environment is not presented to the Congress and the American public, the force will again languish on a shoestring budget. This society is facing one of the greatest domestic challenges to its well-being since the Great Depression. The last item people are interested in is even reasonably sized armed forces. Military service budgets are going to decline because now it appears national defense rests more with resolving domestic ills: budget deficits, the economy, jobs, education, the homeless, national health insurance, immigration, decaying transportation system, civil rights, urban blight, crime and drugs than with preparing to fight an enemy or enemies unknown. It is time to rethink the Army's role in society, the way the Army does business, and the need to face up to radical Army restructuring to meet the 21st century.

ENDNOTES

1. The International Institute of Strategic Studies, *The Military Balance, 1991-1992*, London: Brassey, 1991, pp. 108-109.

2. General Frederick M. Franks, Jr., Memorandum for BG Grogan, ADCSCD, SUBJECT: The Army in the Post-Cold War Era. Fort Monroe: TRADOC, February 18, 1992.

3. Interview with LTC Avihai Tzihor, IN, IDF, U.S. Army War College, Carlisle Barracks, PA, November 20, 1991.

4. Samuel Rolbant, *The Israeli Soldier: Profile of an Army*, New York: Thomas Yoseloff, 1970, p. 85.

5. Reuven Gal, *A Portrait of the Israeli Soldier*, Westport,CT: Greenwood Press, 1986, pp. 11 and 12.

6. Rolbant, pp. 99-102; Ian V. Hogg, *Israeli War Machine*, London: Quarto Publishing, LTD, 1983, pp. 26-32.

7. Gal, p. 11; The International Institute of Strategic Studies, *The Military Balance, 1991-1992*, London: Brassey, 1991, pp. 108-109.

8. Ze'ev Schiff, *A History of the Israeli Army*, New York: Macmillan Publishing Co., 1985, pp. 102-103.

9. Gal, pp. 30-33.

10. Tirza Leibowitz and Michael Stein, *IDF Journal*, "A Time to Study, A Time To Serve," No. 16, Winter 1989, pp. 39-41.

11. Yigal Allon, *Massach Shel Hol*, pp. 276-277, quoted in Edward Luttwak and Dan Horowitz, *The Israeli Army*, New York: Harper and Row, 1975, p. 82.

12. Luttwak and Horowitz, p. 85.

13. Luttwak and Horowitz, p. 87; Gal, p. 127.

14. Schiff, p. 106; Gal, pp. 115-128.

15. *Ibid*; Luttwak and Horowitz, pp. 87, 116.

16. Gal, p. 128.

17. Luttwak and Horowitz, p. 182; J.F.C. Fuller, *Generalship, Its Diseases and Their Cure*, Harrisburg,PA: Military Service Publishing Co., 1936.

18. John C. Sparrow, *History of Personnel Demobilization in the United States Army*, Washington: GPO, 1952, p. 139; Gal, pp. 37-38.

19. Schief, p. 108.

20. *Ibid*, p. 109.

21. Gal, p. 124.

22. *Ibid*, pp. 116-125.

23. Luttwak and Horowitz, pp. 75, 79; Rolbant, pp. 82-83; Gal, pp. 39, 42.

24. Gal, pp. 87-88, 92-94; Rolbant, pp. 82-83.

25. International Institute for Strategic Studies, *The Military Balance, 1981-1982*, quoted in Gal, p. 43; Luttwak and Horowitz, p. 78; Gal, pp. 39, 179, and 233; Rolbant, p. 87.

26. Luttwak and Horowitz, pp. 180-181.

27. Luttwak and Horowitz, pp. 424-425; Gal, p. 39.

28. Gal, pp. 34, 42-43 and 139; Rolbant, pp. 83 and 96.

29. Rolbant, p. 83.

30. Rolbant, p. 83.

31. "Breaking Cliches: Interview: O/C Women's Corps Brig. Gen. Hedva Almog," *IDF Journal*, No. 21, Fall 1990, pp. 30-35.

32. "Miscellaneous," *IDF Journal*, No. 22, January-February 1991, p. 5.

33. *Ibid*.

34. Ibid; Jack Katzenell, "Women Soldiers in Non-Traditional Military Roles," *IDF Journal*, No. 21, Fall 1990, pp. 46-51.

35. Hedva Almog, "Expectations and Possibilities," *IDF Journal*, No. 21, Fall 1990, pp. 36-37.

36. International Institute For Strategic Studies, *The Military Balance 1991-1992*, pp. 108-109; Hogg, pp. 30 and 82.

37. Trevor N. Depuy, *Elusive Victory*, New York: Harper and Row, 1978, pp. 586-587.

38. International Institute for Strategic Studies, *The Military Balance 1991-1992*, p. 109.

39. *Ibid*; Hogg, pp. 94-104.

40. Hogg, *Israeli War Machine*, pp 89-94, International Institute for Strategic Studies, *The Military Balance 1991-1992*, p. 109.

41. "Israel Unveils Its Homemade Tank," *IDF Journal*, No. 17, Summer 1989, pp. 10; Zvi Volk, "Tanks Lead the Way," *IDF Journal*, No. 20, Summer 1990, pp. 19-26.

42. For more on the dysfunctional perceptions between the components and suggestions to more fully integrate the Total Force, see the following SSI publications: Philip A. Brehm, *Restructuring the Army: The Road to a Total Force*, Carlisle, PA: U.S.Army War College, 1992; Gary L. Guertner, ed., SSI Special Report, *The Total Army: Shaping the Active and Reserve Component Relationship*, Carlisle, PA: U.S. Army War College, 1991; Charles E. Heller, SSI Special Report, *Total Army Cadre Integration Study*, Carlisle, PA: U.S. Army War College, 1991; David E. Shaver, *Closing Ranks: The Secret of Army Active and Reserve Component Harmony*, Carlisle, PA: U.S. Army War College, 1992.

43. U.S. Government, *Constitution of the United States*, Article I, Section 8.

44. William B. Johnston, *Workforce 2000, Work and Workers for the Twenty-first Century*, Indianapolis: Hudson Institute, 1987, p. xxi.

45. Interview with Anthony Gough and Frank Martinez, California Conservation Corps, San Bernadino Center, September 4, 1991.

46. Roderick L. Vawter, *Industrial Mobilization: The Relevant History*, Washington: National Defense University, 1983, pp. 90-91.

47. Hogg, p. 91.

48. David Ben Gurion, *Memoirs*, New York: The World Publishing Co., 1970, pp. 66-105, quoted in Gal, p.12.

49. Edward M. Coffman, *The Old Army*, New York: Oxford University Press, 1986, p. 39-40.

50. Larry I. Bland, *The Papers of George Catlett Marshall*, Vol. 1, "The Soldierly Spirit," December 1880-June 1939, Baltimore: The Johns Hopkins University Press, 1881, p. 393.

51. U.S. Executive Branch, "Remarks by the President at the Address to the Aspen Institute Symposium," Aspen, CO: The Aspen Institute, August 2, 1990.

52. Luttwak and Horowitz, pp 181-182.

53. U.S. War Department, War Department Circular No. 347, *Military Establishment*, Washington, DC: GPO, August 25, 1944.

54. Eric C. Ludvigsen, "Lessons for Today in Desperate Stand 42 Years Ago," *ARMY Magazine*, Vol. 42, No. 2, February 1992, p. 9.

55. Clay Blair, *The Forgotten War*, New York: Random House, 1987.

U.S. ARMY WAR COLLEGE

Major General William A. Stofft
Commandant

******

STRATEGIC STUDIES INSTITUTE

Director
Colonel Karl W. Robinson

Author
Colonel Charles E. Heller

Editor
Mrs. Marianne P. Cowling

Secretary
Mrs. Ruth S. Bovee

******

Composition
Daniel B. Barnett

www.ingramcontent.com/pod-product-compliance
Lightning Source LLC
Chambersburg PA
CBHW080913170426
43201CB00017B/2314